丝绸之路国际博物馆联盟
首届联盟大会文集

PROCEEDINGS OF THE FIRST CONFERENCE
OF THE INTERNATIONAL ALLIANCE OF MUSEUMS
OF THE SILK ROAD

王春法　主编

Dr. Wang Chunfa

朝華出版社
BLOSSOM PRESS

首届丝绸之路国际博物馆联盟大会嘉宾合影

Representatives at the First Conference of the International Alliance of Museums of the Silk Road (IAMS)

丝绸之路国际博物馆联盟执行理事会第一次会议代表合影

Members of the IAMS Executive Council

与会代表在首届丝绸之路国际博物馆联盟大会上发言

Participants to the First Conference of the IAMS speak at the conference

首届丝绸之路国际博物馆联盟大会与会代表参观福建博物院

Participants to the First Conference of the IAMS made a visit to Fujian Museum

目　录

CONTENTS

CONTENTS

综 述 ▪
Overview

首届丝绸之路国际博物馆联盟大会综述

为贯彻落实习近平总书记关于"丝绸之路经济带"和"21世纪海上丝绸之路"系列重要讲话精神，加强与"一带一路"沿线国家和地区的文明交流互鉴与民心相通，切实推动文化交流、文化传播、文化贸易创新发展，首届丝绸之路国际博物馆联盟大会于 2018 年 11 月 24 至 25 日在中国福建省福州市成功举办。中国国家博物馆馆长王春法致欢迎辞，中国国家文物局副局长关强、中国文化和旅游部国际交流与合作局副局长朱琦、福州市副市长李春出席并致辞。来自阿塞拜疆国家历史博物馆、柬埔寨国家博物馆、哈萨克斯坦国家博物馆、老挝国家博物馆、缅甸国家博物馆（仰光）、塞尔维亚国家博物馆、蒙古国国家博物馆、白俄罗斯国家历史博物馆等 20 多个国家的 30 多所文博机构代表出席联盟大会。大会取得多项重要成果，得到参会者和媒体的高度评价。现就大会的缘起、大会代表的发言和大会成果，综述如下：

一、缘起

2013 年 9 月和 10 月，中国国家主席习近平在出访哈萨克斯坦和印度尼西亚期间，先后提出共建"丝绸之路经济带"和"21世纪海上丝绸之路"（以下简称"一带一路"）的重大倡议，得到国际社会高度关注。2015 年 3 月，为推进实施"一带一路"重大倡议，让古丝绸之路焕发新的生机活力，以新的形式使亚欧非各国联系更加紧密，互利合作迈向新的历史高度，中国政府特制定并发布了《推动共建丝绸之路经济带和 21 世纪海上丝绸之路的愿景与行动》。2016 年 12 月 29 日，原文化部印发《文化部"一带一路"文化发展行动计划（2016—2020年）》（以下简称《行动计划》），其中重点任务之一就是健全"一带一路"文化交流合作机制。该计划提出成立丝绸之路国际博物馆联盟，与丝绸之路国际剧院联盟、丝绸之路国际图书馆联盟、丝绸之路国际美术馆联盟、丝绸之路国际艺术节联盟等一起形成"五大联盟"，共同发挥机制引领作用。

在此背景下，2017年5月18日，中国博物馆协会"丝绸之路"沿线博物馆专业委员会联合国际丝路之绸研究联盟、丝绸之路国际博物馆友好联盟3个组织，以及亚洲、非洲、欧洲、美洲共计145个（其中国际机构37个，国内机构108个）博物馆机构共同倡议发起丝绸之路国际博物馆联盟（以下简称"联盟"）。在时任中国文化部部长雒树刚、中国国家文物局局长刘玉珠、中国国家文物局副局长关强的见证下，哈萨克斯坦国立中央博物馆馆长阿里木白·纳桑、巴基斯坦国立自然历史博物馆馆长穆罕默德·阿克特·贾维德、坦桑尼亚国家博物馆馆长奥达克斯·马布拉，以及中国博物馆协会"丝绸之路"沿线博物馆专业委员会、国际丝路之绸研究联盟、丝绸之路国际博物馆友好联盟等机构代表共同签署《丝绸之路国际博物馆联盟倡议书》。

2018年6月29日，中国文化和旅游部党组决定将丝绸之路国际博物馆联盟秘书处改设在中国国家博物馆，中国国家博物馆为联盟牵头单位，馆长王春法为联盟理事长。

根据习近平总书记重要指示精神和文化和旅游部《行动计划》工作安排，中国国家博物馆主动作为，2018年7月6日，丝绸之路国际博物馆联盟秘书处调整后第一次工作会议在中国国家博物馆召开，确定联盟发起单位中国博物馆协会、中国丝绸博物馆、福建博物院、西安大唐西市博物馆为副理事长单位。会议讨论决定筹备召开首届联盟大会。中国国家博物馆作为联盟牵头单位，积极履行职责和义务，经过4个多月的紧张筹备，2018年11月24至25日，召集各联盟单位在古代海上丝绸之路的重要肇始地——福州召开首届丝绸之路国际博物馆联盟大会。会议致力于探索在丝绸之路沿线国家和地区开展文化遗产领域的主题展览、信息共享、联合研究、人员交流和人才培养，对推动沿线国家和地区之间的博物馆开展国际合作具有重要促进作用。

二、推动联盟制度建设，探讨丝路主题合作，首届联盟大会成功召开

来自国内外联盟机构 14 位代表分别介绍了各自博物馆的基本情况，同时表达了愿意在中国国家博物馆牵头的丝绸之路国际博物馆联盟框架下，积极支持中国政府提出的"一带一路"倡议，针对世界多极化、经济全球化、社会信息化、文化多样化深入发展给博物馆带来的机遇和挑战，积极开展务实合作，践行"和平合作，开放包容，互学互鉴，互利共赢"的丝路精神。

联盟理事长、中国国家博物馆馆长王春法在欢迎辞中表示，博物馆具有独特的文化联动作用，国际博物馆联盟的建设和发展彰显了同舟共济、权责共担的命运共同体意识。联盟成员加强联合协作，盘活馆藏资源，有利于推进丝绸之路沿线国家和地区在尊重文明多样性、道路多样化和发展水平不平衡等差异的基础上互学互鉴、互利共赢。他倡议，联盟各成员要坚持共建共享、合作共赢，造福沿线各国人民，推动构建人类命运共同体。而作为联盟理事长成员单位的中国国家博物馆，将积极履行好职责和义务，切实发挥好桥梁和纽带作用，建立健全沟通机制，努力搭建合作平台，为联盟做好服务和保障工作。

中国国家文物局、中国文化和旅游部国际交流与合作局、福州市人民政府等相关部门领导出席大会并致辞。

中国国家文物局副局长关强在致辞中首先向与会代表、来宾的到来表达了欢迎之情，并对联盟大会的召开表示衷心祝贺。关强表示，丝绸之路一直是古代东西方之间最为重要的文化交流通道和贸易通道，而今天的丝绸之路早已超越其作为交通线的含义。近年来，中国与丝绸之路沿线国家及国际组织多次合作，反映了中国政府对开展丝绸之路相关遗产保护的高度重视，及承担文化遗产保护的国际责任的积极态度。在首届大会召开之时，希望各联盟成员充分利用联盟平台，继续深化合作，优势互补，共同进步，开拓丝绸之路文明互鉴新渠道。

中国文化和旅游部国际交流与合作局副局长朱琦希望大会为各国博物馆分享资源、交流经验、凝聚智慧、共谋发展提供新机遇，助力各国文化交流与合作继续朝着密切、积极、友善的方向发展，以进一步增强共建"一带一路"的国际影响力和感召力，吸引越来越多的沿线国家积极参与。

福州市副市长李春在致辞中介绍，福州是古代海上丝绸之路的重要肇始地，希望与会嘉宾发表真知灼见，助力福州推动文博事业发展。

塞尔维亚国家博物馆馆长博亚娜·博里奇·布雷斯科维奇在发言中提出，展览应该同时具备教育性和娱乐性，博物馆展览成功的标准应当是观众能否从中获得情感体验，而不是在走出博物馆时仅仅了解到具体事实或其科学原理。

中国丝绸博物馆馆长赵丰分享了中国丝绸博物馆在纺织文物的科学研究、鉴定测试、保护修复等方面的成功经验，以及该馆正在筹备举办"丝路岁月：大时代下的小故事"展览的情况。他向大家发出邀请，参与名为"世界丝绸互动地图"的项目，以致力于在世界范围内对纺织品相关历史资料进行全面、系统的调研，并将资料电子化归档，为将来全球研究丝绸之路纺织品奠定坚实基础。同时，建议联盟设立特殊委员会，专门负责展览、保护、培训等工作。

福建博物院院长吴志跃介绍了福建博物院丰富的海上丝绸之路藏品资源，分享了在举办海上丝绸之路文物联展和丝绸之路相关学术研究方面的成功经验，以及水下文化遗产保护项目的最新进展。

西安大唐西市博物馆馆长王彬在发言中介绍了该馆以丝路文化为中心的建馆理念、藏品特点，以及紧扣丝路主题举办的各项展览和文化活动，并表示将不断强化主题丰富丝路文化内涵，继续与丝绸之路沿线博物馆开展友好馆建设，扩大朋友圈。

时任中国国家博物馆党委书记、副馆长黄振春分享了中国国家博物馆在探索总分馆建设模式、推进智慧博物馆建设、加强传播手段创新、实施策展人制度、推动馆际合作等方面的未来规划，并表示希望与各联盟单位加强展览合作，开展交流培训和联合出版工作。

三、明确未来发展方向，会议成果丰硕

经过两天的交流探讨，在丝绸之路国际博物馆联盟各成员单位代表的广泛参与和共同努力下，大会取得了丰硕成果：

一是讨论并通过了《丝绸之路国际博物馆联盟章程》（以下简称《章程》）。《章

程》明确了丝绸之路国际博物馆联盟的宗旨为积极探索在丝绸之路沿线国家和地区开展文化遗产领域的主题展览、信息共享、联合研究、专业人员交流和人才培养，推动沿线国家和地区之间的博物馆开展国际合作，并加强与各博物馆相关国际机构和组织之间的联系与合作，同时提高社会对跨文化交流合作的关注度和参与度，实现丝绸之路上的民心相通。《章程》还规定了成员申请及退出程序，明确了组织机构由执行理事会、秘书处构成。

二是讨论并签署了《丝绸之路国际博物馆联盟展览合作框架协议》。中国国家博物馆将联合来自 12 个国家的 17 家单位于 2019 年 3 月底在北京举办"文明的交流与互鉴"展（暂定名），同时将以"丝绸之路国家博物馆的功能与使命"为主题举办全球博物馆馆长论坛。

三是召开联盟首届执行理事会，讨论并通过了增加缅甸国家博物馆（仰光）、哈萨克斯坦国家博物馆、阿塞拜疆国家历史博物馆和塞尔维亚国家博物馆 4 个国外副理事长成员单位。

四是启动了丝绸之路国际博物馆联盟网站（www.musesilkroad.com），以期加强联盟成员机构间的信息交流和资源共享，为世界各国博物馆及文化保护机构的合作与沟通提供服务与便利。

五是签署了《联盟大会备忘录》，确定联盟大会每两年举办一次。

六是明确了未来工作计划。

（一）推动展览合作，促进文明交流互鉴。丝绸之路国际博物馆联盟成员单位之间每年至少合作举办一次联展或巡展。

（二）加强人才交流，形成联动发展合力。各成员单位应借助丝绸之路国际博物馆联盟这个大平台，在管理、展览、考古、文保、研究等领域联合开展专业人才培养和学术交流，实现专业人员互访的常态化、制度化。

（三）开展文保和考古合作，共同守护人类文化遗产。联盟成员要携手探索文物科学发掘、保护与修复联动机制，尤其是专项文物保护技术的交流互鉴，提升专业技能和业务水平，加强文物的科学性发掘和预防性保护，联合打击文物走私和非法贩卖，共同保护全人类共有共享的文化遗产。

（四）推广新技术应用和智慧博物馆建设，分享创新发展经验。各联盟成员单位应当利用好丝绸之路国际博物馆联盟网站，加强联盟成员单位藏品的数字化和信息化建设，畅通资源共享、信息发布渠道，推动联盟各博物馆可持续、高质量发展。

（五）加强文创开发合作，实现文物资源转化。联盟成员应依托代表性馆藏资源，加强 IP 授权和文创产品研发合作，并在联盟成员单位间优先授权、宣传和销售，以扩展文物的教化意义和知识价值。

千百年来，"和平合作、开放包容、互学互鉴、互利共赢"的丝绸之路精神薪火相传，推进了人类文明进步，是促进沿线各国繁荣发展的重要纽带，是东西方交流合作的象征，是世界各国共有的历史文化遗产。进入 21 世纪，在以和平、发展、合作、共赢为主题的新时代，面对复苏乏力的全球经济形势，纷繁复杂的国际和地区局面，传承和弘扬丝绸之路精神更显重要和珍贵。

博物馆是保护和传承人类文明的重要殿堂，是连接过去、现在、未来的桥梁，在促进世界文明交流互鉴方面具有特殊作用。联盟理事长王春法倡议，丝绸之路国际博物馆联盟不断强化合作机制、明确合作目标，夯实合作基础，同时，积极适应新形势新变化，加快改革和创新，激发博物馆可持续发展活力，以新的形式使亚欧非各国联系更加紧密，互利合作迈向新的历史高度。新时代，新起点，新使命。与会联盟代表一致表示要勇于担当，开拓进取，用实实在在的行动推动联盟工作不断取得新进展，为构建人类命运共同体注入强劲动力。

中国国家博物馆
国际联络部

欢迎致辞 ■
Welcome Speech

在首届丝绸之路国际博物馆联盟大会开幕式上的欢迎辞

丝绸之路国际博物馆联盟理事长、中国国家博物馆馆长　王春法

很高兴与大家相聚在有"福"之地——福建福州，召开首届丝绸之路国际博物馆联盟大会。

福建泉州出土的宋代古船是世界上最早的木质海船之一，见证了中国人民对海洋的勇敢探索。我们的先辈扬帆远航，穿越惊涛骇浪，闯荡出连接东西方的海上丝绸之路。福建是海上丝绸之路的重要起点，也是中国面向世界的主要开放窗口。

2013年，中国国家主席习近平提出共建"一带一路"的倡议，将中国梦同沿

线各国人民的梦想结合起来，赋予古代丝绸之路以全新的内涵。以"和平合作、开放包容、互学互鉴、互利共赢"为核心的丝绸之路精神，打开了各国友好交往的新窗口，书写了人类发展进步的新篇章。

随着世界多极化、经济全球化、社会信息化、文化多样化深入发展，机遇和挑战共存，世界经济增长、普惠平衡发展、弥合贫富差距鸿沟，等等都是需要我们共同面对和思考的问题。

一直以来，文化交流可以促进世界文化繁荣，增进世界和平。作为保护和传承人类文明的重要殿堂，博物馆在促进世界文明交流互鉴方面具有特殊作用。

2017 年 5 月 18 日，在中国国家文物局的指导下，我们联合国内外 145 个文博机构成立"丝绸之路国际博物馆联盟"。联盟致力于探索在丝绸之路沿线国家和地区开展文化遗产领域的主题展览、信息共享、联合研究、人员交流和人才培养。此次大会，我们将讨论并通过联盟章程、展览合作框架协议和 4 家副理事长成员单位，共同签署首届联盟大会备忘录，共同探讨未来合作计划。

今天，来自世界各地的文博机构代表共聚一堂，共商新时代博物馆发展大计，对发挥博物馆独特的文化联动作用，具有重要意义：

一是推进和平合作。丝绸之路见证了沿线各国人民的善意和友谊，架起了东西方合作的纽带，和平的桥梁。国际博物馆联盟的建设和发展顺应了全球治理体系变革的内在要求，彰显了同舟共济、权责共担的命运共同体意识。

二是推进开放包容。文明在开放中发展，民族在融合中共存。不同历史和国情，不同民族和习俗，孕育了不同文明，使世界更加丰富多彩。我们要以文明交流超越文明隔阂、文明互鉴超越文明冲突、文明共存超越文明优越。

三是推进互学互鉴。丝绸之路不仅是一条通商易货之道，更是一条知识交流之路。我们要在尊重文明多样性、道路多样化和发展水平不平衡等差异的基础上相互学习、相互借鉴，取长补短、共同提高。

四是推进互利共赢。丝绸之路见证了陆上"使者相望于道，商旅不绝于途"的盛况和繁华，创造了沿线国家和地区大发展大繁荣。我们应当积极行动起来，加强联合协作，盘活馆藏资源，实现互利共赢。

丝绸之路国际博物馆联盟为促进人类文明交流互鉴，促进民心相通提供了新思路新方案。我们要坚持共建共享、合作共赢，造福沿线各国人民，推动构建人类命运共同体。

作为联盟理事长成员单位，中国国家博物馆将积极履行好职责和义务，切实发挥好桥梁和纽带作用，建立健全沟通机制，努力搭建合作平台，为联盟做好服务和保障工作。

千秋福韵开境界，丝路帆远创新篇。此次大会的胜利召开，标志着丝绸之路国际博物馆联盟建设已经迈出了坚实步伐，只要我们乘势而上、顺势而为、携手努力，沿线国家和地区博物馆之间的合作必将硕果累累。

预祝首届联盟大会取得圆满成功。祝各位来宾在福州度过愉快的时光！

开幕致辞 ■
Opening Speeches

在首届丝绸之路国际博物馆联盟大会开幕式上的致辞

中国国家文物局副局长　关强

　　首先，我代表国家文物局对参加首届丝绸之路国际博物馆联盟大会的各位来宾表示热烈的欢迎！对联盟大会的召开表示衷心的祝贺！

　　起始于古代中国，连接亚洲、非洲、欧洲的丝绸之路，是古代商贸的重要通道和文明交往的桥梁。20 世纪中叶，前苏联考古学家在阿尔泰山脉古代游牧民族墓葬里即发现了精致的中国刺绣鞍褥面，其花纹和工艺都与我国长沙楚墓出土的丝织品高度一致。这表明，至少在公元前5世纪丝绸就开始走出中国、走向世界。西汉时期，我国打通了中原与中亚、西亚及欧洲的交通，形成了一条横亘欧亚大陆的丝绸贸易通道，并在汉魏隋唐时期达到全盛。此后，丝绸之路一直是古代世界东西方之间最为重要的贸易和文化交流通道。今天丝绸之路早已超越其作为交通线的含义，我国国家主席习近平提出共建"丝绸之路经济带"和"21世纪海上丝绸之路"的倡议，已得到国际社会的高度关注和有关国家的积极响应，对进一步加快我国对外开放步伐，促进地区及世界和平发展具有重大意义。

中国政府高度重视并积极开展丝绸之路相关遗产保护，相关遗址已列入世界遗产名录的遗产点。中国与沿线国家以及国际组织合作，建立丝绸之路遗产地保护和博物馆联盟等合作机制，赴沿线肯尼亚、沙特、印度、孟加拉国、乌兹别克斯坦等国开展联合考古调查；在境内外联合举办"丝绸之路""海上丝绸之路""茶马古道""北方草原丝绸之路"等多个大型系列展览；长期参与沿线国家的文化遗产保护援助工程。中国利用位于故宫博物院的国际博协培训中心，先后举办面向东盟和非洲国家的文化遗产保护和博物馆专业人员培训班，积极承担文化遗产保护的国际责任。

加强博物馆领域的国际交流合作，是丝绸之路沿线国家及国际组织的共同责任和愿望。在原文化部、国家文物局支持下，2017年"5·18国际博物馆日"期间，由中国博物馆协会倡议，整合中国博协"丝绸之路"沿线博物馆专委会、丝绸之路博物馆友好联盟以及国际丝路之绸研究联盟等组织，发起成立丝绸之路国际博物馆联盟。后根据需要，联盟改由中国国家博物馆具体联络。我们希望各联盟成员充分利用现有平台，继续深化合作、优势互补、共同进步，开拓丝绸之路文明互鉴新渠道。我们期待各联盟成员在文物展览、藏品管理、学术研究、人员培训、联合考古、社会教育、公共服务、文化产业发展等方面，全方位开展务实交流与合作，多出合作成果。中国国家文物局、中国博物馆协会也将积极支持和促成各项合作。

今天由中国国家博物馆牵头召开首届联盟大会，我们期待看到"一带一路"沿线国家博物馆间的合作由此开启新局面，呈现新气象。祝愿联盟各成员能够在今天的大会上碰撞出合作的火花，预祝本次大会取得圆满成功。

在首届丝绸之路国际博物馆联盟大会开幕式上的致辞

中国文化和旅游部国际交流与合作局副局长　朱琦

　　非常高兴和各位相聚在福州，共同参加首届丝绸之路国际博物馆联盟大会。在此，我谨代表中华人民共和国文化和旅游部，对本次大会的召开表示热烈的祝贺！

　　陆上丝绸之路是以西安为起点，经中亚、西亚并连接地中海各国的陆上通道。海上丝绸之路形成于秦汉时期，繁荣于唐宋时期，是古代中国与外国交往最早的海上通道。古丝绸之路不仅是一条通商易货之道，更是一条知识交流之路。在历史发展过程中，沿着古丝绸之路，中西文化碰撞、交流、融合，不断激发出新的火花，在人类文明史上书写出"使者相望于道，商旅不绝于途"的华彩篇章。

2013 年 9 月和 10 月，习近平主席在分别出访哈萨克斯坦和印度尼西亚期间，先后提出共建"丝绸之路经济带"和"21 世纪海上丝绸之路"的重大倡议，旨在共同打造政治互信、经济融合、文化包容的利益共同体、命运共同体和责任共同体。我们重提丝绸之路，坚持合作共赢，倡导交流互鉴，不仅源于世界各国人民对于全球化合作重要性认识的不断提高，更是出于各国人民对历史长河中丝绸之路所发挥作用的广泛认同。从 2013 年到现在，共建"一带一路"借用古丝绸之路的历史符号，高举和平发展的旗帜，由理念变为行动，由愿景转化为现实，在世界范围内广受欢迎和响应。

福建自古是中国东南沿海地区与海外经济文化交流活动最为频繁的地区之一，作为重要的货运港口被世界公认为海上丝绸之路的起点。今天，我们在这里召开首届丝绸之路国际博物馆联盟大会，具有十分重要的意义。2017 年 5 月 18 日，为全面推进"一带一路"文化建设，切实发挥沿线国家文化机构的机制引领作用，丝绸之路国际博物馆联盟正式成立，至今已有 110 家境内成员、47 家境外成员积极参与。联盟网站今天正式上线，将为世界各国博物馆及文化保护机构的合作与沟通提供服务与便利。

今天，首届丝绸之路国际博物馆联盟大会隆重举行，将继续传扬"和平合作、开放包容、互学互鉴、互利共赢"的丝绸之路精神，进一步增强共建"一带一路"的国际影响力和感召力，吸引越来越多的沿线国家积极参与进来。希望联盟各成员单位秉持共商、共建、共享原则，进一步加强交流合作，以文明交流超越文明隔阂、文明互鉴超越文明冲突、文明共存超越文明优越，为切实增进民心相通、造福沿线各国人民做出积极贡献。

再次感谢各位代表的光临。预祝此次联盟大会取得圆满成功。祝大家在福州度过愉快的时光！

在首届丝绸之路国际博物馆联盟大会开幕式上的致辞

中国福建省福州市人民政府副市长　李春

　　昨天，第八届中国博物馆及相关产品与技术博览会顺利开幕。今天上午，我们在此召开首届丝绸之路国际博物馆联盟大会，为丝路沿线国家博物馆搭建沟通交流的平台，推动彼此进一步深化合作、共赢发展。受福州市人民政府尤猛军市长委托，我谨代表福州市人民政府，向首届丝绸之路国际博物馆联盟大会的顺利召开表示热烈的祝贺！向出席本次大会的各位领导、各位专家表示衷心的感谢！

　　福州历史悠久，是古代海上丝绸之路的重要肇始地。史料证明，早在汉代，福州就与中南半岛、日本等地开通了交通航线。五代王审知及其家族主闽时期，积极推进与朝鲜、日本及东南亚、阿拉伯地区进行贸易往来。明代，郑和七下西洋船队都在长乐太平港驻泊，并以此作为扬航的基地。明清时期，中国与琉球朝贡贸易主要通过福州进行。福州参与创造了古代海上丝绸之路的历史辉煌，在中西商贸往来和文化交流史上具有突出地位，至今还留存有众多的海丝史迹。2012 年 11 月 17 日，我市有 6 处海丝文化遗产点列入中国世界文化遗产预备名单，这是我市文化遗产首次列入中国世界文化遗产预备名单。

长期以来，在国家文物局的关心支持下，福州市委、市政府高度重视海丝文化遗产保护、利用与申遗工作，专门成立了由市政府市长担任组长的申报世界文化遗产工作小组，加入了海丝保护和申遗城市联盟，公布实施了《海上丝绸之路福州史迹文化遗产保护管理办法》和《福州市海上丝绸之路史迹保护条例》，建成并对外免费开放了福州市海上丝绸之路展示馆等。当前，我市正全力加快推进"海上福州"建设，已连续举办多届海上丝绸之路旅游节、丝绸之路国际电影节、21 世纪海上丝绸之路博览会等大型活动，持续深入开展"福州品牌海丝行"，进一步推进与海丝沿线城市的互联互通、市场开拓、人文交流等，积极打造海丝核心区建设的战略支点。我们衷心希望，各位专家在首届丝绸之路国际博物馆联盟大会上擦出思想火花、提出真知灼见，为广大文博工作者带来深刻启迪和崭新思路，同时也为我们提出良好的意见和建议，帮助我们进一步推动全市文博事业发展，推动福州做好海丝保护、利用和申遗工作！

最后，祝首届丝绸之路国际博物馆联盟大会圆满成功。

大会发言 ▪
Conference Papers

阿塞拜疆国家历史博物馆

丝绸之路国际博物馆联盟副理事长

阿塞拜疆国家历史博物馆馆长　纳伊拉·瓦利克哈诺娃

　　阿塞拜疆国家级博物馆的起源与阿塞拜疆国家历史博物馆的成立紧密相连。国家历史博物馆于 1920 年奠基，同年 6 月 15 日正式成立，1936 年前名为阿塞拜疆国家博物馆，是阿塞拜疆首个国家博物馆，也是阿塞拜疆的科学教育中心。

　　阿塞拜疆国家历史博物馆致力于收藏和保存从古至今能够反映阿塞拜疆人民物质和精神追求的藏品，并对其进行展示、研究和出版。目前，博物馆共有来自各个历史时期的藏品约 30 万件。

博物馆位于阿塞拜疆首都巴库，曾为阿塞拜疆石油大亨、慈善家和社会公众人物哈吉·泽纳拉宾·塔吉耶夫（1838—1924）的宅邸。该建筑建于 1895—1901 年，在阿塞拜疆总统伊尔哈姆·阿利耶夫的倡议和支持下于 2005—2007 年进行了翻修。博物馆内至今仍设有塔吉耶夫的纪念馆。

博物馆内设有 11 座藏品库房，考古学、民族志、钱币学等 6 个研究部门，以及文物修复实验室和图书馆等。这些部门的研究人员在各个时期发表了诸多作品，包含着最丰富的博物馆研究资料；博物馆通过出版书籍、宣传册、图录、画册、学术刊物等，让更多读者得以了解博物馆藏品的丰富信息。博物馆每年出版的学术性出版物包括《阿塞拜疆国家历史博物馆》《阿塞拜疆国家科学院阿塞拜疆国家历史博物馆》指南，另外还有大量图录、画册及其他出版物，包括《阿塞拜疆国家历史博物馆藏宝石》《卡拉巴赫地毯》《巴库、舍尔万和库巴地毯》等。

阿塞拜疆国家历史博物馆与俄罗斯、土耳其、美国、德国、中国、挪威、梵蒂冈、捷克等多个国家的博物馆及研究机构建立了合作关系，广泛参与展览、会议、论坛等国际活动，并开展共同研究和人员交流，曾在日本、挪威、捷克等国举办巡回展览。

阿塞拜疆国家历史博物馆在举办丝绸之路展览方面有很多成功经验，并开展了许多历史学研究。19 世纪至 20 世纪，丝绸之路对阿塞拜疆产生了巨大影响。阿塞拜疆国家历史博物馆收藏有许多古代丝绸之路沿途贸易流传下来的丝织品，以及其他与丝绸之路有关的东、西方文物。在古代，来自中国和印度的商品经丝绸之路来到阿塞拜疆，对当时的贸易产生了重大影响。13 世纪至 15 世纪，中国和阿塞拜疆互派使者，文化、经济交流持续增多。博物馆的藏品中就有许多经考古发现来自中国的外销陶器、家具、茶具等。在当时，从中国和其他东亚国家进口的餐具、丝绸、珠宝、武器等广受欢迎，已经成为人们日常生活中不可或缺的产品。由于中世纪制作瓷器的技术难度较大，从中国进口的瓷器，具有鲜明的中式特征，因而在阿塞拜疆首都广受欢迎且价格昂贵。

在 18、19 世纪，各国的历史彼此紧紧相连，商业贸易和文化交流极大地丰富了人民的生活。总而言之，丝绸之路对阿塞拜疆产生了深远影响。未来，阿塞拜疆国家历史博物馆将继续探索历史遗迹，不断发掘不同文明相互交融的例证。

纳伊拉·瓦利克哈诺娃

丝绸之路国际博物馆联盟副理事长
阿塞拜疆国家历史博物馆馆长

　　历史学博士、国际博物馆协会会员，2007年当选院士。其研究领域包括中世纪阿塞拜疆历史渊源研究、阿拉伯哈里发地区研究、社会经济关系、政治文化史以及历史地理学等。她打破了亚美尼亚和格鲁吉亚在地区历史编纂学领域占据主导的格局，并取得重大研究进展。曾发表和出版超过248篇（部）文章和书籍，其中19篇（部）在国外发表和出版；多次参加国内和国际会议，并获数次表彰及奖励。

哈萨克斯坦国家博物馆

哈萨克斯坦国家博物馆副馆长　萨图巴尔丁·阿拜·卡雷姆塔叶维奇

　　哈萨克斯坦国家博物馆期待与国外各大博物馆和主办方博物馆建立密切的合作关系，增进与丝绸之路沿线博物馆的合作。

　　作为实施国家项目"文化遗产"的一部分，哈萨克斯坦国家博物馆于 2014 年 7 月 2 日对外开放，是全国最年轻、规模最大的博物馆。博物馆总面积 7.4 万平方米，展览面积 1.4 万平方米，共有 10 个固定展厅和 6 个临时展厅，讲述了哈萨克斯坦从古至今的历史。其中，考古学展厅展示了哈萨克斯坦丰富的历史文化；独立哈萨克斯坦展厅展示了哈萨克斯坦走向独立发展的心路历程；阿斯塔纳展厅通过重要文物和文献展示了阿斯塔纳时期国家的发展和文化；现代艺术展厅则通过不同流派的当代艺术、视觉艺术以及一些雕塑品，形象地展示了哈萨克斯坦在现代化进程中的文化变迁。

博物馆现有员工 531 人，共有 14 个部门，包括研究所、修复工作室和实验室、图书馆等。博物馆共有藏品 20 余万件，其中包括斯基泰 - 塞卡时期的七个"黄金勇士"。

国家博物馆是哈萨克斯坦首都最受欢迎的文化遗产之一。开馆四年来，累计参观人数已超过 300 万人次。博物馆每年举办大量的国际和国内文化活动，包括展览、会议、论坛、讲座、博物馆课程、节日活动和圆桌会议等。

众所周知，古代的丝绸之路途经哈萨克斯坦。丝绸之路作为东西方交流的桥梁，连接着许多中世纪的城市，比如塔拉兹、突厥斯坦等，这些也都是哈萨克斯坦境内的知名城市。哈萨克斯坦考古学家在丝绸之路沿线中世纪城市的考古发现展示了各国之间的文化合作与交流，其中的许多文物就收藏在哈萨克斯坦国家博物馆中。

在哈萨克斯坦、中国、吉尔吉斯斯坦跨国联合申报的"丝绸之路：长安—天山廊道的路网"项目中，哈萨克斯坦有 8 处遗迹列入联合国教科文组织的世界遗产名录。作为该项目的一部分，2017 年在香港历史博物馆举办的"绵亘万里—世界遗产丝绸之路"联合展览通过来自哈萨克斯坦、中国和吉尔吉斯斯坦博物馆的展品，专门展示了丝绸之路上的历史遗迹。

最后，就与丝绸之路国际博物馆联盟的合作与发展问题发表一点意见。哈萨克斯坦国家博物馆再次重申希望与各方增进合作的意愿，并且已做好准备加入丝绸之路国际博物馆联盟。关于对联盟工作的建议，哈萨克斯坦国家博物馆希望继续推进传统形式的馆际合作，比如为年轻的博物馆专业人员组织研讨会及培训活动，共同开展科学研究、策划联合展览和会议等活动。

萨图巴尔丁·阿拜·卡雷姆塔叶维奇

哈萨克斯坦国家博物馆副馆长

教育背景：

2000 年至 2004 年	就读于列·尼·古米列夫欧亚国立大学，主修考古学与民族学，以优异成绩毕业
2003 年至 2004 年	通过了列·尼·古米列夫欧亚国立大学军事部门的考核，获预备中尉军衔
2006 年至 2008 年	就读于列·尼·古米列夫欧亚国立大学，主修考古学与民族学，以优异成绩毕业并获得硕士学位
2009 年 9 至 10 月	在俄罗斯圣彼得堡国立文化艺术大学完成"文化领域的国家政策"短期主题研究
2010 年至 2012 年	就读于哈萨克斯坦共和国总统公共管理学院，以优异成绩毕业并获公共与地方行政管理硕士学位
2011 年 6 月	在美国杜克大学斯坦福公共政策研究所实习

工作经历：

2004 年至 2005 年	总统文化中心　高级研究员，首席策展人
2005 年至 2007 年	哈萨克斯坦第一任总统博物馆　高级研究员
2007 年至 2008 年	哈萨克斯坦文化信息部历史文化遗产司　首席专家
2008 年至 2014 年	哈萨克斯坦文化部文化委员会　首席专家
2014 年至 2015 年	哈萨克斯坦文化与体育部文化艺术司　首席专家
2015 年至今	哈萨克斯坦国家博物馆　副馆长

柬埔寨国家博物馆

柬埔寨国家博物馆馆长　孔·维列

　　柬埔寨国家博物馆坐落于柬埔寨首都金边市，是柬埔寨历史上第一座博物馆。最初设想的博物馆功能并不仅局限于保存和展示藏品。在成立之初，它就与柬埔寨艺术学院比邻而居，学院以培训各类手工艺人为主要任务，两者相得益彰。这也是柬埔寨国家博物馆的创始人乔治·格罗利埃（George Groslier）的愿景，他认为艺术在长时间的休眠后变得有些不太敏锐，但仍旧具有强大潜能，而古代文物正好能够为现代艺术提供灵感。而这也恰恰是在参观 19 至 20 世纪的日常生活物品时，观众仍然能感受到其艺术价值的原因。从事珠宝制作、金属铸造、绘画、雕塑、编织的学徒们在一个极为有利的氛围中工作。有必要提及的是，古代文物开始陆续从其原址失踪，入藏世界各地，而对这些文物的法律保护及控制措施却并不明确。由此，组建博物馆势在必行。

1917 年，柬埔寨国家博物馆第一块基石庄严奠基，博物馆施工项目随即启动，1920 年竣工并举行落成典礼，当时被命名为"阿尔伯特萨罗特博物馆"。暂且不论其第一批藏品如何，该建筑本身就是一件杰出作品，这一点得到了广泛认同。

1951 年，法国将文化遗产的管辖权移交至高棉当局，博物馆也随之更名为"柬埔寨国家博物馆"。然而，博物馆馆长一直由法国人担任，直到 1966 年才出现第一任柬埔寨馆长。

建馆至今，柬埔寨国家博物馆一直致力于收藏考古和民族学藏品，石器、木器、金属器、陶瓷等各类藏品不断丰富，与藏品相关的一系列导览、图录和出版物等相继出版，为大众所知。

柬埔寨国家博物馆所收藏的史前、前吴哥、吴哥与后吴哥时期的雕塑、陶瓷及民族学藏品是世界上最伟大的高棉文化遗产之一，主要包括印度教和佛教相关的石制、木制和金属雕塑，以及陶瓷、民族学藏品、纺织品、绘画和礼器等。

柬埔寨国家博物馆的藏品丰富，跨越不同历史时期，包括前吴哥时期（5、6 世纪至 8 世纪末期）、吴哥时期（9 世纪至 14 世纪晚期）、后吴哥时期（15 世纪到 19 世纪中期），以及 19 世纪后受西方艺术影响的现代艺术风格。在柬埔寨国家博物馆的青铜展厅中，既有 6 米高的 11 世纪塑像，也有跪坐女性像和装饰佛等。石像展厅展出了 6 世纪初期印度教、佛教和基督教的宗教雕像，并陈列有 10 世纪晚期的湿婆、雪山神女像及 13 至 14 世纪的阎王像。木雕和民族学展厅主要展示 18 至 19 世纪晚期的藏品，包括木雕装饰品和雕像等。绘画展厅的陈列以 19 世纪末期的画作为主，它们受法国殖民主义的影响，但又与西方绘画不尽相同，保留了柬埔寨传统画像技法。

对于柬埔寨国家博物馆与丝绸之路国际博物馆联盟之间的关联，也许大家会存有疑问，即柬埔寨的艺术品和手工艺品能否反映丝绸之路这一主题。尽管中国历史文献已反复证明两国曾互派使者并建立了外交关系，但中柬之间的联系和交往比较抽象。柬埔寨文明受印度和中国的影响较深，其中印度的影响是显见的，体现在从艺术到建筑，从宗教到王权，从语言到哲学等各方面；然而，中国对柬埔寨的影响却是潜在的，除了大量进口的中国陶瓷之外，很难在高棉文明中看到中国图像或元素，其他影响可以从交易系统、计算、测量等方面找到蛛丝马迹，令人印象深刻。对于柬埔寨国家博物馆来说，用藏品展现与丝绸之路的联系虽然存在一定困难，但也有迹可循。例如，巴戎寺藏有一面 13 世纪的浮雕，画面表现了一艘中国商船及其主人。可以看出，船上坐着数位中国人，其头饰、衣装与当地人皆不相同，可以推测为到柬埔寨做生意的中国商人。

以上就是柬埔寨国家博物馆的基本情况。柬埔寨有大量中国唐、明两代的文物和遗迹，以及一些来自中国福建的艺术藏品，柬埔寨国家博物馆希望未来可以与中国举办更多的交流展览。

孔·维列

柬埔寨国家博物馆馆长

　　现任柬埔寨文化艺术部博物馆司司长，兼任柬埔寨国家博物馆馆长。毕业于柬埔寨金边皇家艺术大学考古系，获得考古学学士学位。曾就读于巴黎的法国高等社会科学院（EHESS）并于1998年获得文化人类学硕士学位。1998至2005年，曾与日本政府吴哥保护团队一起在吴哥工作。2005年至2012年，曾任皇家美术大学教育服务主任，后任副校长一职。2012年11月，任文化艺术部博物馆司司长。

老挝国家博物馆

老挝国家博物馆馆长　佩玛莱婉·乔本玛

　　老挝国家博物馆坐落于老挝首都万象，博物馆所在建筑是老挝现存最古老的殖民建筑之一。该建筑最早修建于1925年，在1975年老挝独立前，一直被皇家政府用于举办会议和仪式，后于1980年设立展厅，1985年成为老挝革命博物馆，2000年更名为现在的老挝国家博物馆。2017年12月1日，在庆祝老挝成立42周年国庆之际，老挝国家博物馆举行了新馆开馆仪式。

　　老挝国家博物馆收藏了超过 28,000 件已登记文物和约 130,000 件尚未登记的文物，包括绘画、石器、铜制品、木制品、铁制品、瓷器等。博物馆亦收藏有反映丝绸之路历史的杯具、玉器等藏品。

　　老挝国家博物馆讲述本国从史前时代至今的历史，重点关注文化历史和自然环境。博物馆是了解老挝的窗口，藏品覆盖面广泛，老挝国民得以借此保护和发展老挝集体记忆。自 2000 年以来，每年数以千计的国内外游客、学者和学生前来老挝国家博物馆参观。

　　由于旧馆储存空间有限，老挝政府决定修建新馆。新馆邻近老挝前总统宅邸、老挝国家图书馆及老挝国立大学。建筑共三层，设有五个展览主题，分别为：史前时代、澜沧王国、现代历史、政府的开发和保护举措、老挝的民族。新馆投入使用后制订了新的展览计划，并根据展览主题和内容需要审慎选择展品。在新馆筹备期间，博物馆邀请了日本的考古学家和历史学家来老挝举办讲座、研讨会，并参与历史遗迹考察。

　　未来，老挝国家博物馆将充分利用新馆重新安置并妥善保存国家收藏，培训博物馆员工，升级现有展览，举办新展览以提升观众体验。同时，博物馆将更新藏品存储设备，升级文物保护实验室以更好地保存藏品。博物馆还设立了外国奖学金和其他合作项目以支持学术研究和博物馆发展。老挝国家博物馆希望加强与所有友好伙伴联系，特别是向经验丰富的博物馆学习，以期改善未来工作。与此同时，也希望能够和丝绸之路国际博物馆联盟的众多博物馆交流工作经验。

佩玛莱婉·乔本玛

老挝国家博物馆馆长

教育背景：

1982 年至 1987 年　俄罗斯奥里奥尔大学文学硕士（M.A）

职业经历：

1987 年至 1990 年　老挝信息文化与旅游部外事局

1990 年至今　　　　老挝国家博物馆 馆长

参与项目：

MuSEA 项目老挝展览专家组成员，该项目由东南亚博物馆合作项目 SIDA（老挝、越南、柬埔寨和瑞典）赞助。

缅甸国家博物馆（仰光）

丝绸之路国际博物馆联盟副理事长

缅甸国家博物馆（仰光）馆长 杜楠劳宁

　　缅甸共有 30 多家博物馆，其中包括国家博物馆、考古博物馆、纪念馆、宗教博物馆、地区博物馆、专题博物馆和私人博物馆，均属文化和宗教事务部管理。费尔博物馆是缅甸首家博物馆，成立于 1871 年，蒲甘遗址博物馆、妙乌遗址博物馆先后落成于 1902 年和 1905 年。

　　1948 年缅甸独立后，缅甸国家博物馆（仰光）于 1952 年 6 月成立，历经1968 年、1993 年两次迁址后，于 1996 年 9 月 18 日在仰光市卑谬路 66/74 号重新对外开放。缅甸国家博物馆（仰光）是一栋 5 层建筑，近 25 米高，占地面积 7000 平方米，展厅面积 1.8 万平方米。博物馆共有 13 个展厅，主展厅为象征权力和力量的狮子王座展厅，展出了 1957 年皇室移交而来的八个古代缅甸国王王座的模型和一个末代君主王座原件。

缅甸的文化政策是保存多元文化遗产，包括物质文化遗产和非物质文化遗产。作为国家博物馆，缅甸国家博物馆（仰光）以收集、保护并展示缅甸文化遗产为己任，致力于成为公众了解缅甸文化及文明进程的中心，通过保护缅甸的文化遗产以塑造更美好的未来。博物馆现有收藏、博物馆财产的保存与保护、研究与出版、展览（常设展与临时展）、公共教育等五项职能。

缅甸国家博物馆（仰光）现有藏品 70 余万件。根据缅甸的国家政策，国家博物馆肩负着收藏各类文物，以及绘画作品、手工艺品的责任。藏品主要通过购买、捐赠、移交、交换、拍卖等方式获得，以当地人民或文物机构捐赠为主。

基于保护国宝的原则，博物馆不仅着眼于本馆藏品、区域保护、藏品编目调查、文物收集、有形文化遗产登记，还与联合国教科文组织和东盟等国际组织建立了联系，举办各种活动。

缅甸国家博物馆（仰光）通过研究和出版向学校和公众传播信息，这是很重要的博物馆职能。研究分主题开展，以图录、手册和书籍等形式出版研究成果。报告、指南、宣传册等形式的出版物可以让人们更加了解博物馆及其活动。特殊展览、周年纪念之际的专门出版物可以提升博物馆在社区中的知名度。本馆通过开展一系列关于文物和文化的培训课程，传播缅甸文化。2002 年起，缅甸的大学中开始设立博物馆课程。

作为本馆最重要的职能之一，展览在国际文化传播方面起着重要作用。根据文化交流计划，本馆曾与其他国家合作举办众多展览。值得一提的是，缅甸国家博物馆（仰光）曾于 2005 年 6 月举办"缅中建交 55 周年纪念展"。此外，博物馆还举办许多本地展览，也曾经承担国家任务举办联合国日展览等。

为进一步健全博物馆组织结构，改善博物馆现状，缅甸国家博物馆（仰光）在缅甸文化和宗教事务部的管理与领导下，与国内其他部门和机构开展广泛合作，同时积极寻求其他国家的先进技术支持。自古以来，缅中联系密切，文化是两国友好交往的桥梁，两国的合作对世界文化交流做出了贡献。未来两国博物馆可以通过签署合作备忘录，开展艺术交流、展览交换、人员培训、举办儿童教育项目等，继续加深合作。希望两国在博物馆界更加紧密地交流与合作，成为东盟国家的楷模。

杜楠劳宁

丝绸之路国际博物馆联盟副理事长
缅甸国家博物馆（仰光）馆长

教育背景：

2009 年	缅甸仰光国立文化艺术大学 博物馆学 学士
2017 年	缅甸仰光国立文化艺术大学 博物馆学 硕士

职业经历：

1992 年至 2015 年　缅甸掸邦文化博物馆（东枝） 二级策展人、主任、助理馆长、副馆长、馆长

2015 年至今　　缅甸国家博物馆（仰光） 馆长

学术成果：

联合国教科文组织共同体财产名录研讨会，缅甸掸邦娘水，2014 年

新加坡培训学校公共政策与行政改革课程，2015 年

联合国教科文组织非物质文化遗产名录缅甸提名候选人培训课，缅甸东枝，2015 年

联合国教科文组织 2005 年《公约》认证研讨会，缅甸内比都，2017 年

基本外交技能培训课，缅甸仰光，2017 年

以色列文物局

以色列文物局博物馆及展览部主任　奥丽特·沙米尔

　　以色列是一个非常年轻的国家，全国约有 350 个考古博物馆、展览及户外展览，其中一些拥有数十年历史。随着国家发展，以色列进行了大量考古发掘，但博物馆的藏品仍然有限，有时需要向政府、公共机构，甚至酒店、医院等借用展品进行展示。

　　本次会议对以色列的博物馆具有重要意义。我们的博物馆正在探寻采用新的方式向公众展示文物并阐释其内涵，特别是在教育年轻一代方面希望有所创新。

　　以色列是个小国家，博物馆和国家机构的联系非常紧密。以色列文物局与世界各地博物馆交往密切，曾多次向其他国家的博物馆出借文物，与中国的博物馆也保持着良好的合作关系。

　　通过本次会议，本人结识了来自中国以及丝绸之路国际博物馆联盟的诸多同事和朋友，对此深感荣幸。

丝绸之路国际博物馆联盟首届联盟大会文集

奥丽特·沙米尔

以色列文物局博物馆及展览部主任

哲学博士（耶路撒冷，2007 年），现任以色列文物局博物馆及展品部主任兼有机材料策展人。专业领域为新石器时代至中世纪时期以色列的古代纺织品、织布机、纺轮等。多次应邀在学术和公共活动中发表演讲和论文。其著述及论文清单详见于 antiquities.academia.edu/OritShamir。

白俄罗斯国家历史博物馆

白俄罗斯国家历史博物馆考古、钱币和兵器部主任　卢达·托尔卡切娃

　　白俄罗斯国家历史博物馆是白俄罗斯最大的博物馆，藏品逾 46 万件，涉及 58 个门类。博物馆的历史最早可追溯至 1919 年，几经更名，1992 年改名为"白俄罗斯国家历史和文化博物馆"，2009 年改名为"白俄罗斯国家历史博物馆"并沿用至今。二战时期，博物馆的藏品受到了一些损坏。二战后，藏品被转移到德国，之后只有约 2% 的小部分藏品回到本国，馆藏规模受到重创。

2014 年，5 家机构成为白俄罗斯国家历史博物馆的分馆，包括：俄国社会民主工党一大会址纪念馆、白俄罗斯戏剧音乐文化历史博物馆、白俄罗斯电影历史博物馆、现代白俄罗斯国家制度博物馆和白俄罗斯自然生态博物馆。每家分馆均设有展厅，独立举办常设展厅，并自主开展文化和教育活动。

白俄罗斯国家历史博物馆的主要活动为：博物馆资金的获取，财务管理，博物馆藏品、科学和辅助材料的保存和修复；临时展览的筹备和开放，分馆内常设展览的改陈；对于博物馆藏品、科学和辅助材料的研究、使用和普及；为博物馆观众提供参观服务、文化和教育服务，以及举办文化和教育活动；参与并举办科学和实用性研讨会、会议，以及博物馆业务领域的其他活动；组织国际文化项目；推进方法学工作，为当地历史和自然历史类地区博物馆提供咨询服务。

白俄罗斯国家历史博物馆的藏品中有一部分是从丝绸之路沿线国家的考古发现所得，主要包括珠宝、生活器具、瓷器、钱币和武器等。这些藏品大部分从未对外展出过。希望通过丝绸之路国际博物馆联盟的平台促进我馆与中国及其他丝路国家的交流与发展，有更多的机会合作举办文化交流展览，向中国及世界各地的观众展示白俄罗斯丰富的文化遗产。

卢达·托尔卡切娃

白俄罗斯国家历史博物馆考古、钱币和兵器部主任

教育背景：

2002 年至 2007 年	白俄罗斯国立大学历史系 美术学士学位
	（侧重于装饰与实用艺术、教堂器皿）
2008 年至 2009 年	白俄罗斯国立艺术学院 硕士课程 艺术学硕士学位
	（侧重于白俄罗斯宗教用途的金属艺术品）
2009 年至 2012 年	白俄罗斯国立艺术学院 研究生课程
2016 年	白俄罗斯国立艺术学院 艺术批评哲学博士

工作经历：

2010 年至今	白俄罗斯国家历史博物馆
2016 年至今	白俄罗斯国家历史博物馆 考古、钱币和武器部主任
2018 年至今	白俄罗斯国家历史博物馆 博物馆董事会成员

学术兴趣：

白俄罗斯金属艺术、白俄罗斯钱币学、十六至十七世纪白俄罗斯领土范围内的国际金融关系

参与出版物：

参加过约 20 次国际和国内会议，包括：2018 年在白俄罗斯明斯克举办的纪念瓦伦丁·里亚布谢维奇教授的第三届科学读物会议，2017 年在白俄罗斯明

斯克拉乌比齐举办的第八届国际钱币学大会，2017 年在俄罗斯维利基诺夫哥罗德举办的第十九届全俄罗斯钱币会议。

在同行评审期刊和文章科学摘要中发表过 17 篇论文，包括《十七世纪下半叶至十八世纪上半叶波兰立陶宛联邦和普鲁士硬币之苏哈鲁斯基典藏》（俄语），发表于《银行公告杂志》，第二期；《白俄罗斯国家历史博物馆十六世纪上半叶波兰立陶宛联邦和西欧硬币之布罗多克典藏》（俄语），载于《纪念瓦伦丁·里亚布谢维奇教授的第三届科学读物会议文章摘要》，明斯克，2018 年；《从罗马银币到白俄罗斯卢布：白俄罗斯国家历史博物馆钱币展》（俄语），载于《第十九届全俄罗斯钱币会议文章摘要》，莫斯科，2017 年。

俄罗斯斯塔夫罗波尔考古所

俄罗斯斯塔夫罗波尔考古所高级研究员　兹韦兹达娜·多德

　　俄罗斯斯塔夫罗波尔考古所建立于 1995 年，是一所专业研究机构，包括历史文化古迹的考古研究、开发建设区域内的历史文化古迹的认定、文物和考古纺织品的保护、考古研究地理信息技术的开发与部署等。

　　丝绸之路横贯欧亚大陆，起始于中国，途径俄罗斯，远达欧洲。在丝绸之路沿线俄罗斯境内发现了包括丝绸制品在内的许多中国文物。俄罗斯众多文博机构同中国的文博机构以丝绸之路、丝绸之路沿线藏品，以及丝绸之路考古为主题共同开展了多个研究项目，如俄罗斯斯塔夫罗波尔考古所和中国丝绸博物馆合作进行了蒙古纺织品鉴定修复项目等。这些合作项目包括一些既有项目，也取得了崭新的研究成果。俄罗斯的文博机构也参与到丝绸之路相关的国际组织之中，本研究所曾数次积极参与国际丝路之绸研究联盟组织的国际会议。第三届国际丝路之绸研究联盟研讨会于2018年11月在韩国扶余成功召开，第四届联盟学术研讨会将于2019年9月在俄罗斯举行，届时本研究所将承办该研讨会，艾米塔什博物馆也将作为协办单位参加。

衷心欢迎并邀请各位专家代表对俄罗斯斯塔夫罗波尔考古所及我们的研究和合作给予更多关注与支持。

兹韦兹达娜·多德

俄罗斯斯塔夫罗波尔考古所高级研究员

研究领域：

中亚和北高加索地区的中世纪服饰及纺织品

教育背景：

俄罗斯科学院东方学研究所　博士

斯塔夫罗波尔国立大学　考古学硕士

斯塔夫罗波尔国立大学　历史学、教育学学士

工作经历：

1980 年至 1982 年　斯塔夫罗波尔国立档案馆档案管理员

1987 年至 1997 年　斯塔夫罗波尔国立博物馆考古部主任

1994 年至 1997 年　斯塔夫罗波尔国立博物馆考古部策展人

1997 年至 2010 年　斯塔夫罗波尔国立大学考古学与艺术史教授

2011 年至 2018 年　俄罗斯科学院南方科学中心高级研究员

2018 年至今　　　　俄罗斯斯塔夫罗波尔考古所高级研究员

俄罗斯北高加索地区古代史与考古研究所高级研究员

变革——塞尔维亚国家博物馆

丝绸之路国际博物馆联盟副理事长

塞尔维亚国家博物馆馆长　博亚娜·博里奇·布雷斯科维奇

　　塞尔维亚国家博物馆是塞尔维亚规模最大、历史最悠久的博物馆。该馆成立于1844年，其前身是塞尔维亚博物馆。二战结束后，1950年搬入国立抵押银行。经过短暂修缮，博物馆于1952年面向公众重新开放。2015至2018年博物馆再次对银行建筑进行了彻底改造，开启了发展的新篇章。

　　塞尔维亚国家博物馆是一家综合性博物馆，主要致力于通过考古、钱币和艺术收藏来保护、诠释和促进巴尔干半岛中部以及欧洲从史前到现代的文化遗产多样性。博物馆依循预防性保护原则收藏和保存文物，诠释历史和当代文化，是知识传播源泉和大众学习中心。

塞尔维亚国家博物馆一直是巴尔干地区最重要的博物馆学中心、国家和地区博物馆的模范。此外，还应成为具有地区和世界重要性的国家文化中心，塞尔维亚人民和世界游客必到的游览目的地。

塞尔维亚国家博物馆重视激发和鼓励人们的好奇心。在这里，常设展览代表共同能量，是一种集体创造性活动，不同领域的专家各司其职、发挥所长；同时，它也是一个公众区域，从研究、保护到诠释、教育等各种博物馆活动均在这里发生。全新的常设展览将博物馆最具价值、最引人入胜的考古、钱币、艺术藏品呈现在观众眼前。

最新的常设展览旨在通过独特的方式诠释文物在历经历史洗礼之后的长期价值，并为博物馆观众提供探究的机会，通过时间顺序呈现该地区文化和历史发展的连续性及不连续性，展现文化联系及其相互交织与渗透，展示博物馆最有价值、最吸引人的考古、钱币和艺术等30个门类的收藏，按照时间顺序从地理、艺术、文化、社会、科学等方面进行展示，希望鼓励、传达并培养观众对道德和审美价值的感受，帮助观众提高对自我身份的认知，陶冶情操，并提高对过去的认知。

衡量博物馆展览成功的标准应当是观众能否从中获得情感体验，获取新的态度或兴趣点，而不是在走出博物馆时仅仅了解到具体事实或其科学原理。展览应该同时具备教育性和娱乐性，其目的在把参观者的兴趣、态度、价值观或情绪转变为探索展品的全新价值与意义，而这一切则植根于参观者对展品真实性的信任。

博物馆藏品跨越了50万年历史，其中包括公元前7千年的诸神雕像、公元前5—6世纪温查雕像、公元前13—16世纪战车、公元前6世纪的黄金面具和青铜箱、4世纪的贝尔格莱德浮雕和君士坦丁大帝青铜头像、12世纪的米罗斯拉夫福音书、13世纪的拉多斯拉夫钱币、中世纪东正教壁画及圣像、15世纪的珐琅瓷片，很多塞尔维亚和南斯拉夫艺术家的作品，诸如19世纪的乌罗什·普列蒂奇和帕夫莱·约万诺维奇，20世纪的娜代日达·彼得罗维奇、萨瓦·舒曼诺维奇和伊万·梅斯特罗维奇等人，以及卡巴乔、鲁本斯、德加、雷诺阿、马蒂斯、毕加索、蒙德里安等大师杰作。

　　通过创新的展览呈现方式，塞尔维亚博物馆展现了对考古和艺术史的理解，代表着当今塞尔维亚及其周围地区从史前到中世纪晚期文明的发展与变化，展示了重要的艺术倾向和风格，以及中世纪至今，本国和欧洲的最高艺术成就和杰出作品，创造了新的考古学和艺术思维方式，重新思考塞尔维亚的民族身份，以新的方式去审视和理解我们所生活的世界。

　　古往今来，地处巴尔干半岛的塞尔维亚不断发展，成为人文融合和交织的地方。数世纪以来，塞尔维亚一直是地区间文化交流的场所，被视为东西方、亚洲和欧洲之间的桥梁。

　　如今，人员、信息和商品的流通比以往任何时候都更加迅速。塞尔维亚国家博物馆希望通过通俗易懂的方式诠释历史、延续传统，在 21 世纪，也将一如既往成为知识传递和文化融合的道路与桥梁。

博亚娜·博里奇·布雷斯科维奇

丝绸之路国际博物馆联盟副理事长
塞尔维亚国家博物馆馆长

　　毕业于贝尔格莱德大学哲学系，主修古典学，兼修考古学，获得该系历史学部硕士学位。在塞尔维亚国家博物馆工作期间，任博物馆顾问、策展人。1994 年至 1996 年，曾任贝尔格莱德市文化局局长；1996 年至 2001 年首次任塞尔维亚国家博物馆馆长；其后，担任博物馆策展人；2012 年再次任塞尔维亚国家博物馆馆长。布雷斯科维奇的研究领域为古代巴尔干半岛中部的文化史和经济史，其研究成果曾多次在欧洲其他博物馆和研究机构发表。她还曾组织或参与组织过多次展览及其他活动，并在一些科研项目中与他人合作或负责领导科研团队。

中国梦的启航之地——中国国家博物馆

丝绸之路国际博物馆联盟秘书长、中国国家博物馆副馆长　黄振春

　　中国国家博物馆是代表国家收藏、保管、研究、展示和阐释能够充分反映中华优秀传统文化、革命文化和社会主义先进文化代表性物证的最高机构，珍藏着民族集体记忆和国家优秀文化基因。140万余件藏品呈现和见证着中国人民历史与现实的记忆和对未来的美好愿景，年平均接待观众量近800万人次。作为国家的文化客厅，中国国家博物馆肩负着传播和弘扬中华文化、促进中外文化交流的重要作用。

自 2011 年新馆正式开放运行以来，中国国家主席习近平 5 次到中国国家博物馆参观并发表重要讲话。中国国家博物馆也是中国国家主席习近平首次提出中国梦的地方。

2018 年，中国国家博物馆完成了复兴之路新时代部分、马克思诞辰 200 周年和改革开放 40 周年大型展览等中央交办的任务。此外，还举办了"俄罗斯国家历史博物馆藏十月革命文物展""美国 19 世纪专利模型展""无问西东——从丝绸之路到文艺复兴展""澳大利亚树皮画艺术家展"等国际交流展。年初，我馆到韩国国立中央博物馆参加了合作展览，今年 12 月还将到塞尔维亚国家博物馆举办"文心万象——中国古代文人绘画与生活"展。

关于中国国家博物馆的未来发展方向，我们有这样几方面的规划：

一是探索总分馆建设。博物馆总分馆建设是大势所趋，也是推动博物馆向高质量发展的重要机遇。通过总分馆结合的方式盘活展览文物资源，实现博物馆总分馆管理体系和运行机制的创新，有利于促进文化、文物和旅游协调发展。目前，中国国家博物馆已确定在中国雄安新区和深圳筹建分馆，各项工作稳步推进。

二是推进智慧博物馆建设。中国国家博物馆提出了建设智慧博物馆的目标任务，将通过大数据、云计算、物联网、虚拟现实、人工智能等现代科技手段，让文物活起来。与此同时，推动博物馆的管理和服务信息化、智能化水平实现跨代跃升。

三是加强传播手段创新。互联网时代，中国国家博物馆将不断加强传播手段和方式创新，加强多媒体内容建设，提高新闻舆论的引导力、影响力和公信力。提高用有特色的方式方法讲有特色的故事的能力。强化博物馆公共教育职能，扩大和提升陈列展览的社会效应。

四是实施策展人制度。策展人制度不仅仅是人才政策，更是博物馆领域一场深刻的体制机制变革。中国国家博物馆将通过实施策展人制度进一步推动把展览这个博物馆主责主业抓紧抓好，突出展览功能。

五是推动馆际合作。中国国家博物馆将按照"开放合作、互利共赢，不求所藏、但求所展"的原则，加强与地方博物馆的沟通联络，建立战略伙伴关系，促进借展和重要展览巡展的常态化、制度化和机制化；继续加大与国外文博机构特别是各国国家博物馆的合作力度，开展国际巡展，举办国际论坛，推动交流互鉴。

博物馆是保护和传承人类文明的重要殿堂，是连接过去、现在、未来的桥梁，在促进世界文明交流互鉴方面具有特殊作用，而丝绸之路国际博物馆联盟就是在持续放大这种特殊作用。

自2018年6月丝绸之路国际博物馆联盟秘书处改设在中国国家博物馆以来，在大家的共同努力下，我们进一步明确了丝绸之路国际博物馆联盟秘书处的工作职责、工作机制和职责义务，起草了《丝绸之路国际博物馆联盟章程》，建起了丝绸之路国际博物馆联盟网站。这些工作为今天大会的顺利召开奠定了良好的基础。

2019年，丝绸之路国际博物馆联盟将着重做好以下几方面工作：

一是加强平台建设。进一步完善联络机制，充分发挥好秘书处的协调作用，确保合作项目的延续和深入。

二是加强展览合作。陆续举办以"文明的交流与互鉴"为主题的"一带一路"国家博物馆联合展览、全球博物馆馆长论坛、丝路岁月展览、丝绸之路博物馆策展人论坛等展览和论坛等活动。

三是开展交流培训。根据各联盟成员单位需求，有目的、有针对性地派遣专业人员互访，围绕特定主题深入开展交流与培训活动，相互启迪，共享学术资源与成果。

四是开展联合出版。充分利用各联盟成员单位藏品和人才资源优势，开展共同研究，联合出版学术著作。

"却好五云最深处，闲鸥威凤共联盟。"往后，大家就是好伙伴、好朋友。中国人说有缘千里来相会。今天来自国内外的文博同行相聚在这里，正是一种跨越地域的不解之缘，让我们珍惜缘分，深化友谊，共同为推进世界文明，增进人类福祉贡献更大力量。

黄振春

丝绸之路国际博物馆联盟秘书长
中国国家博物馆副馆长

教育背景：

    1983 年 7 月　毕业于天津南开大学政治经济学专业

工作经历：

    1983 年 7 月至 1992 年 12 月　教育部、国家教育委员会干部

                            国务院办公厅副处级秘书

                            中共中央宣传部办公厅副处级秘书

    1992 年 12 月至 1996 年 7 月　中共中央宣传部办公厅正处级秘书

                            文化部办公厅正处级秘书

    1996 年 7 月至 2005 年 7 月　文化部办公厅副主任

    2005 年 7 月至 2009 年 2 月　文化部办公厅主任

    2009 年 2 月至 2019 年 2 月　中国国家博物馆党委书记、副馆长

丝绸之路沿线的国际合作 —— 中国丝绸博物馆

丝绸之路国际博物馆联盟副理事长、中国丝绸博物馆馆长　赵丰

　　中国丝绸博物馆于 1992 年建成开放，是一个年轻的博物馆，简称"国丝馆"。中国丝绸博物馆有多处馆舍，包括丝路馆、桑蚕馆、织造馆、修复馆、时装馆等。

　　其中，丝路馆主要展示中国丝绸历史。织造馆主要展示中国传统桑蚕丝织技艺。这种技艺已于 2009 年被列入世界非物质文化遗产名录。此外，博物馆中还设有养蚕室和采桑园。

　　为促进纺织文物的科学研究、鉴定测试、保护修复，中国丝绸博物馆于 2000

年 10 月成立了中国纺织品鉴定保护中心。该中心自成立以来，已在纺织品文物的分析检测、修复保护、制作工艺和信息收集及规范研究等方面开展了许多卓有成效的工作，并取得了一系列成果。该中心不仅对中国的博物馆，也对丝绸之路沿线国家博物馆提供文物保护方面的支持。

修复馆中设有纺织修复工作室和展示区，主要展出纺织文物修复方面的展览。

时装馆专门展示中国及西方时装的变迁，并举办一系列临时展览和特别展览，2016 年我馆从韩国、日本、俄罗斯、印尼、印度、欧洲等地商借藏品，举办"锦绣世界：国际丝绸艺术展"，展示世界各地精彩纷呈的丝绸文物。2018 年，我馆举办"神机妙算：世界织机与织造艺术"展览，展出非洲、美洲、亚洲与欧洲种类各异的纺织机及丰富多样的纺织品。

三年前，国际丝路之绸研究联盟 (IASSRT) 成立，成员包括来自 17 个国家的 30 多家机构及多位著名学者。联盟成立以来，通过召开大会、举办展览等形式促进丝绸之路相关学术研究。2016 年，中国丝绸博物馆主办了第一届国际丝路之绸研究联盟大会、研讨会及配套时装展。2017 年，第二届国际丝路之绸研究联盟研讨会于法国里昂举办，来自不同地区的 40 余位参会学者进行了为期两天的讨论，分享具有当地特色的丝绸文化。第三届国际丝路之绸研究联盟研讨会于 2018 年 11 月在韩国扶余举办，与会者 100 余人。在为期两天的研讨会后，与会学者赴首尔实地参观调研韩国国立中央博物馆及纺织工作室等多处机构。第四届学术研讨会将于 2019 年 9 月在俄罗斯召开，研讨会将由俄罗斯斯塔夫罗波尔考古所承办，国立艾尔米塔什博物馆协办。第五届研讨会计划于 2020 年 11 月 5 日至 11 月 15 日在意大利召开。中国丝绸博物馆期待更多组织和机构的加入。

在联盟工作计划方面，中国丝绸博物馆策划了一个名为"世界丝绸互动地图"的项目，邀请所有成员参与。该项目致力于在世界范围内对纺织品相关历史资料进行全面、系统的调研，并将资料电子化归档，为将来全球研究丝绸之路纺织品奠定坚实基础。中国丝绸博物馆计划于明年在西班牙举办相关学术研讨会，希望邀请更多成员加入此项目。

在接下来五年中，丝绸之路国际博物馆联盟将和成员一起制定规划并推进合作。中国丝绸博物馆 2019 年将举办"丝路岁月：大时代下的小故事"特别展览。

该展览受同名图书《丝路岁月——从历史碎片拼接出的大时代和小人物》启发而策划。该书作者魏泓（Susan Whitfield）描述了士兵、商人、僧侣等丝绸之路沿途形形色色的人物，通过这些时代不同、民族不同、身份不同的人留下的历史碎片重塑丝路岁月。展览分为三部分：第一部分"草原丝绸之路"介绍两个不同部族的故事；第二部分"沙漠丝绸之路"与生活息息相关，内容非常丰富，描绘了丝路沿线驿站的小吏、敦煌将军、神秘贵族、丝路胡商等不同身份人群的服饰、文化、生活习惯、宗教信仰及葬俗；第三部分"海上丝绸之路"着重讲述两个人物的故事，通过福州皇族贵妇"市舶司之女"的精美丝绸服饰反映宋代高超的丝织技艺，通过讲述"南海一号"船主生活的艰辛与乐趣来反映海上对外贸易的盛况。

展览开幕的同时，中国丝绸博物馆还将举办"丝绸之路博物馆策展人论坛：主题与合作"，届时各国博物馆策展人将围绕丝绸之路主题展览合作进行讨论，就丝绸之路展览的策展经验和学术内容进行报告。2019年5月，中国丝绸博物馆计划举办"天然染料双年展"及配套研讨会，介绍世界各地典型染料品种、印染工艺和色彩文化。

针对联盟未来工作，建议丝绸之路国际博物馆联盟设立特殊委员会，专门负责展览、保护、培训等工作。中国丝绸博物馆坐落在杭州，环境优美，设施齐备，可以支持联盟开展培训等活动。

赵丰

丝绸之路国际博物馆联盟副理事长
中国丝绸博物馆馆长

教育背景：

1978 年至 1982 年　浙江丝绸工学院（今浙江理工大学）染整专业，获工学学士

1982 年至 1984 年　浙江丝绸工学院（今浙江理工大学）中国丝绸史方向毕业，获工学硕士

1995 年至 1997 年　中国纺织大学（今东华大学）中国纺织史，获工学博士

职业经历：

现任中国丝绸博物馆馆长、纺织品文物保护国家文物局重点科研基地主任、东华大学（原中国纺织大学）教授、博士生导师、国际丝路之绸研究联盟主席。

学术成果：

发表中英文论文 100 余篇，主笔和主编著作约 20 部，主持国家级、省部级科研课题 10 余项。其中主编的《中国丝绸通史》获中华优秀出版物奖、中国出版政府奖；主编的《敦煌丝绸艺术全集》获国家出版基金；主编的《中国丝绸艺术》英文版获全美纺织品协会 2012 年度 R.L. Shep 纺织品图书奖。

福建博物院

丝绸之路国际博物馆联盟副理事长，福建博物院党委书记、院长　吴志跃

　　福建博物院坐落于福州市西湖公园，在全国省级博物馆中是唯一集博物馆、自然馆、积翠园艺术馆、考古研究所、文物保护中心、国家水下考古基地"六合一"的综合性博物馆。福建博物院曾获得"2016 年全球博物馆及文化遗产保护领域最杰出、最具创新力、最具启发意义项目"奖。2015 年作为全球唯一受邀博物馆参加联合国成立七十周年之际举办的"一带一路"研讨会。此外，福建博物院是唯一在海峡两岸文化产业博览会上蝉联金奖的博物馆。2015 年获得了由中国博物馆协

会颁发的"全国最具创新力博物馆"荣誉称号。

福建博物院的 28 万余件藏品涵盖海上丝绸之路、华人华侨、红色革命等诸多门类。基本陈列"福建古代文明之光"展厅面积 1400 平方米，共展出文物 503 件，包含"石涛十二屏"、林觉民《与妻书》等，在第九届全国博物馆十大陈列展览精品评选中获得"最佳内容设计奖"。

2010 年开始，福建博物院历时 3 年打造"丝路帆远 —— 海上丝绸之路文物精品联展"，该展曾在国内 11 个省区的 24 个城市、国外 20 个国家的 23 个城市展出，并持续至今。该展曾获得"全国十大陈列展览精品奖"，并得到外交部通报表扬。"绿叶对根的情意 —— 华侨华人奉献展"是为了响应国家文物局在全国范围内征集以"弘扬优秀传统文化、培育社会主义核心价值观"为主题的展览的号召而策划的。福建拥有 1860 万华侨，被毛主席誉为"华侨旗帜，民族光辉"的陈嘉庚就出生在福建。基于这个特点，2018 年博物馆策划举办了"华侨旗帜民族光辉 —— 百国百侨百物展"。

学术研究方面，博物馆实施"十大课题""五年计划""百万投入"，鼓励学术研究、科研成果出版。创新服务方面，举办了品牌"双百"活动，每年定期为 100 所高校、100 个居民社区服务。福建博物院还打造了"纸上博物馆""网上博物馆""空中博物馆"和"地铁博物馆"，同时正在为机场打造 2000 平方米"空港博物馆"。

福建博物院在全国开展有 4 个水下文化遗产保护项目，与中国国家博物馆在肯尼亚、西沙群岛进行的水下考古合作超过 20 年。最近几年，平潭水下考古也取得了新进展，有了新的考古发现。

吴志跃

丝绸之路国际博物馆联盟副理事长
福建博物院党委书记、院长

职业经历：

　　文博研究馆员，享受国务院政府特殊津贴。任福建省文物局副局长、福建博物院党委书记、院长。担任中国博物馆协会"丝绸之路"沿线博物馆专业委员会主任、中国博协常务理事。入围"2014中国文化管理年度人物"100强，2015年荣获"全国文化系统先进工作者"称号。担任文化和旅游部及博物馆界高级专业技术职称评委，多次担任国家艺术基金、中国博物馆十大精品陈列展览、中国博物馆设计资质和施工资质、中国博物馆学优秀学术成果奖终评评委。

开展"一带一路"人文交流的实践与探索
——西安大唐西市博物馆

丝绸之路国际博物馆联盟副理事长、西安大唐西市博物馆馆长　王彬

　　大唐西市博物馆是一座年轻的民营博物馆，也是中国第一座民办遗址类博物馆。博物馆由大唐西市文化产业投资集团投资兴建，是一次中国民间资本保护文化遗产、兴建博物馆的探索。大唐西市博物馆是大唐西市文化产业项目的重要组成部分及文化核心。大唐西市国家文化产业示范基地占地面积 500 亩，建筑面积 128 万平方米，总投资 80 亿元；博物馆占地面积 20 亩，建筑面积 3.5 万平方米。博物

馆于 2010 年 4 月 7 日建成并对外开放。开馆以来，一直秉持社会公益性、文化产业性，每年接待观众 60 多万，累计接待观众 500 多万人次，按照国家专业规范，开展社会教育、陈列展览、科学研究等各方面工作。

一、不断强化主题丰富丝路文化内涵

大唐西市博物馆建设在 1400 年前唐都长安城的国际贸易中心之上，即大唐西市。因为是遗址类博物馆，所以博物馆的陈列展览都围绕丝绸之路文化展开。基本陈列"丝路起点 盛世商魂"，重在叙述历史。专题展览"货币中的丝路故事——大唐西市博物馆藏丝路古币展"展出了 1400 多枚来自 47 个国家的古代货币，解读了当时的文化、风土人情和历史内涵。博物馆还利用馆藏丝绸举办了专题展览"丝路锦绣——大唐西市博物馆藏丝绸文物选粹"，其展品一部分出土于大唐西市，一部分是博物馆创办人的收藏捐赠，另一部分则来自社会捐赠和拍卖购得的文物。"丝路聚珍——大唐西市博物馆藏精品文物展"主要通过金银器和陶瓷解读丝路文化，共展出文物 26,975 件。"锦样胡风——大唐西市博物馆藏丝绸文物选粹展"则通过丝绸纹样解读当时丝路上的文化交流。

大唐西市博物馆开馆至今已举办临时展览 76 个，主要以丝绸之路为主题，比如与中国国际友谊博物馆合作的"至尊国礼——丝绸之路沿线友好国家国礼展"，与上海东敦煌禅艺中心共同举办的"丝路明珠·精神净土——丝绸之路沿线佛教石窟壁画临摹展"等。与此同时，大唐西市博物馆还引进了"丝路的故事——陕西皮影展"，通过昭君出塞、张骞出使西域、西游记等皮影故事反映了丝绸之路的文化交流面貌。

博物馆所举办的教育活动紧扣丝路主题。因大唐西市是历史上的贸易中心，博物馆举办了"'变废为宝'我是小小创业家"跳蚤市场活动，以提高儿童的人际交往能力、计算能力和语言能力。活动沿袭了大唐西市当时开市闭市，诚信交易，非常具有仪式感，颇受观众欢迎。展览配套"传承中国影灯 演绎丝路故事"皮影体验活动得到了国内外观众的热烈响应。博物馆在馆内、馆外开展的讲座也多以丝路故事和丝路精神为主题，例如丝路文化进校园进社区宣讲活动，讲解人穿上唐装，讲解唐人的衣食住行。2015 年至 2018 年，与西安高校合作连续四年举办"丝路情·西市杯"大学生讲解风采大赛，2018 年度举办大唐西市博物馆首届"丝路小小讲解员"培训班等，上述文化活动均围绕丝绸之路主题开展，颇受好评。

博物馆的文化产业也延伸了丝绸之路主题。丝路文化体验中心分为展示区、体验区、研学区三个部分，旨在让观众领会古代丝路文化的同时，也能够了解丝绸在现代生活中的运用和历史文化元素中的展现。博物馆举办的"丝路百工体验展"就设置了传统手工业体验活动，观众制作的商品还可进行售卖。

二、开展友好馆建设，扩大朋友圈

自 2013 年中国提出"一带一路"建设倡议后，大唐西市博物馆积极与丝路沿线国家进行友好建设，与吉尔吉斯斯坦、乌兹别克斯坦、蒙古国、哈萨克斯坦、乌克兰等国家的多个博物馆签订友好馆协议。截至目前，大唐西市博物馆已经与丝绸之路沿线 16 个国家共 22 家博物馆建立了友好馆关系，倡议成立了丝绸之路国际博物馆友好联盟，搭建了大唐西市博物馆与丝路沿线国家博物馆之间交流的桥梁。

与此同时，博物馆积极开展与各个博物馆的展览合作。2014 年，在吉尔吉斯斯坦国家博物馆举办"丝路的故事——陕西皮影展"，并于同年引进"19 世纪吉尔吉斯人物质文化展"。2015 年，在哈萨克斯坦国立中央博物馆举办"丝路的故事——陕西皮影展"，并于次年引进反映哈萨克斯坦巧克力历史文化的"奇妙的巧克力世界——世界著名巧克力大师尼古拉作品展"，该展览还得以在宁夏、吉林等多地展出，产生很大影响和社会效益。2018 年，"欧亚大草原早期游牧民族文化——哈萨克斯坦文物精品展"在西安展出，这是哈萨克斯坦国立中央博物馆首次在中国举办文物展览。

大唐西市博物馆还积极利用自身资源，在行业内牵线搭桥。例如，帮助吉尔吉斯斯坦伏龙芝博物馆与八路军西安办事处纪念馆建立联系，促成塔吉克斯坦库洛布共和国博物馆群与陕西省文化遗产研究院在文物修复方面的合作等。

博物馆积极搭建平台，促进人文交流。大唐西市博物馆与陕西省妇联合作，在博物馆建立西安首家"丝绸之路妇女之家"，主要与丝绸之路沿线妇女同胞在人文交流方面开展活动。2016 年 9 月 6 日，我馆牵头成立丝绸之路国际博物馆友好联盟，并召开首届丝绸之路国际博物馆友好联盟大会。联盟现有成员涉及 17 个国家共计 66 家博物馆，其中国际 22 家，国内 44 家。

未来，大唐西市博物馆将全面配合统一部署，依据联盟规划积极开展工作，同时凸显自身优势，继续完善丝绸之路文化展示内容，推进友好馆建设，扩大朋友圈，搭建平台，促进人文交流。希望联盟能够凝聚力量，在做研究中心、展示中心、文创中心、研学中心时有聚有合，各有侧重，同时积极推进"文物 + 数字化 + 互联网"多领域深度融合，构建新型展示、交流新平台。

王彬

丝绸之路国际博物馆联盟副理事长
西安大唐西市博物馆馆长

教育背景：

历史学硕士

职业经历：

1981 年起从事文博工作至今，曾任陕西历史博物馆副馆长，现任西安大唐西市博物馆馆长、理事会副理事长，陕西历史博物馆研究员，中国国家文物局评审库专家。中国文物协会纺织专业委员会副主任、中国博协丝绸之路专业委员会副主任、丝绸之路国际博物馆联盟副理事长、丝绸之路国际博物馆友好联盟主席、中国文物学会理事、陕西省博物馆协会理事、西安市博物馆协会副主任委员。

学术成果：

主编《解读国宝》丛书（四卷）、《陕西的辉煌与梦想》《陕西历史博物馆》《古都明珠、华夏宝库》《历史上的大唐西市》《西安大唐西市博物馆》等书籍；在唐代妇女服饰和民办博物馆理论实践方面成果丰富。

闭幕致辞 ■
Closing Speech

首届丝绸之路国际博物馆联盟大会闭幕词

丝绸之路国际博物馆联盟理事长、中国国家博物馆馆长　王春法

　　经过一天半的会议，在丝绸之路国际博物馆联盟各成员单位代表的广泛参与和共同努力下，我们实现了丝绸之路国际博物馆联盟网站的正式上线，讨论并通过了《丝绸之路国际博物馆联盟章程》和 4 家副理事长成员单位，共同签署了《丝绸之路国际博物馆联盟展览合作框架协议》及《联盟大会备忘录》，确定了下一届联盟大会召开的时间和地点，圆满完成了各项既定议程。

　　此次大会开放、务实、富有成效。大家分享了本国博物馆发展成就和经验，并针对世界多极化、经济全球化、社会信息化、文化多样化深入发展给博物馆带来的

机遇和挑战，提出了思考，发表了建议，探寻了路径。

新时代，我们应共享未来。令人欣慰的是，大家在博物馆领域就践行"和平合作，开放包容，互学互鉴，互利共赢"的丝路精神达成了共识。大家一致认为在当前世界经济形势下，丝绸之路国际博物馆联盟致力于探索在丝绸之路沿线国家和地区开展文化遗产领域的主题展览、信息共享、联合研究、人员交流和人才培养，对推动沿线国家和地区之间的博物馆开展国际合作具有重要促进作用。下面，我想就丝绸之路国际博物馆联盟未来的发展谈几点建议：

第一，推动展览合作，促进文明交流互鉴。我们要进一步加强联系与协作，丝绸之路国际博物馆联盟成员单位之间每年至少合作举办一次联展或巡展。由相关成员单位联合策展，以展示多元文明，让沿线国家地区博物馆丰富的馆藏文物都活起来，不断提高社会公众对跨地域、跨文化交流合作的关注度和参与度，促进丝绸之路各国民心相通，加强世界文明交流互鉴。展览和巡展期间举办学术论坛，及时回应联盟成员单位共同关注的重点、难点和热点话题。

第二，加强人才交流，形成联动发展合力。人才是应对未来挑战的核心。各成员单位应借助丝绸之路国际博物馆联盟这个大平台，一道推进人才交流与合作向纵深发展，在管理、展览、考古、文保、研究等领域联合开展专业人才培养和学术交流，实现专业人员互访的常态化、制度化。中国国家博物馆愿意每年与各成员单位互派3～5名急需专业中青年专家学者，开展交流合作和业务培训。建议从2019年起，联盟成员每年分领域、分主题至少进行一次研讨交流。2019年的主题是：新时代与战略发展，将由中国国家博物馆主办。往后，欢迎各成员单位积极承办相关主题活动。

第三，开展文保和考古合作，共同守护人类文化遗产。全球博物馆在文物保护和考古的政策法规、历史沿革、科技条件等诸多方面存在差异，联盟合作应有利于各博物馆之间优势互补，取长补短。下一步，联盟成员要携手探索文物科学发掘、保护与修复联动机制，尤其是专项文物保护技术的交流互鉴，提升专业技能和业务水平，加强文物的科学性发掘和预防性保护，联合打击文物走私和非法贩卖，共同保护全人类共有共享的文化遗产。应以人类探源工程、人类迁徙路线图等基础研究作为重要方向，探索丝绸之路沿线国家地区的文物和文化内在关联性，积极开展联合考古。

第四，推广新技术应用和智慧博物馆建设，分享创新发展经验。 在日新月异的信息化社会，科技创新已成为博物馆未来发展的新引擎。目前，中国国家博物馆正在全力推进"智慧国博"建设，我们愿意同各联盟成员一道共同探讨智慧博物馆发展的新方向，互相优先提供智力和技术装备支持，发挥大数据、云计算、3D 打印、AR 等新技术在博物馆藏品保护、展览陈列、社会教育等方面的积极作用。利用好丝绸之路国际博物馆联盟网站，加强联盟成员单位藏品的数字化和信息化建设，畅通资源共享、信息发布渠道，推动联盟各博物馆可持续、高质量发展。

第五，加强文创开发合作，让文物活起来，实现文物资源转化。 在"博物馆热"的全球背景下，集合传统和时尚元素的文创产品越来越多地受到人们追捧，成为传播文物知识、传递审美价值、拉近观众与博物馆距离的重要载体。中国国家博物馆重视文创产品研发，推出了众多广受好评的产品。联盟成员应依托代表性馆藏资源，加强 IP 授权和文创产品研发合作，并在联盟成员单位间优先授权、宣传和销售，以扩展文物的教化意义和知识价值。以博物馆藏品和平台为依托，策划时装周、体育节、动漫节、音乐节、影视节等方面的文化交流展示活动。

思路决定出路。我们要通过丝绸之路国际博物馆联盟的平台，不断强化合作机制、明确合作目标，夯实合作基础。与此同时，我们还意识到要积极适应新形势新变化，加快改革和创新，激发博物馆可持续发展活力，努力推动构建人类命运共同体。

女士们，先生们，朋友们！乘风破浪会有时，直挂云帆济沧海。新时代，新起点，新使命，我们要勇于担当，开拓进取，用实实在在的行动推动联盟工作不断取得新进展，为构建人类命运共同体注入强劲动力。

难忘福州！在会议闭幕之际，再次向大家表示感谢。感谢各成员单位为筹备和举办此次大会所做出的努力。我们期待 2020 年联盟成员在北京再次相聚！

论坛成果

Achievements

成果文件 1：

丝绸之路国际博物馆联盟
首届执行理事会备忘录

在《丝绸之路国际博物馆联盟章程》框架下，首届丝绸之路国际博物馆联盟执行理事会会议于 2018 年 11 月 24 日在中国福州召开，联盟理事长、副理事长及秘书长共 6 人参加会议，达成以下共识：

一、通过讨论，各成员一致同意新增 4 家副理事长单位加入执行理事会。具体名单为：

    1. 缅甸国家博物馆（仰光）

    2. 哈萨克斯坦国家博物馆

    3. 阿塞拜疆国家历史博物馆

    4. 塞尔维亚国家博物馆

二、第二届丝绸之路国际博物馆联盟大会将于 2020 年 11 月在北京举行。

此后每两年召开的联盟大会由有能力举办的成员单位轮流主持，具体召开时间和议程将由各成员单位协商，协商结果由联盟秘书处通知各成员。

执行理事会成员签字：

理事长　王春法

秘书长　黄振春

副理事长　安来顺

副理事长　赵丰

副理事长　吴志跃

副理事长　王彬

2018 年 11 月 24 日

中国福州

成果文件 2：

首届丝绸之路国际博物馆联盟大会
备忘录

在《丝绸之路国际博物馆联盟章程》框架下，首届丝绸之路国际博物馆联盟大会于 2018 年 11 月 24 至 25 日在中国福州召开。来自亚洲、欧洲、非洲 12 国的 17 家成员单位参加会议。各成员单位就联盟章程文件、未来合作方向等诸项事宜进行了讨论，并达成以下共识：

一、联盟成员确认丝绸之路国际博物馆联盟是一个丝绸之路沿线国家和地区在博物馆领域的非政府性、非营利性的、开放的国际合作组织和交流平台。联盟成员一致同意秉持以和平合作、开放包容、互学互鉴、互利共赢为核心的丝绸之路精神，开展多方面合作与交流。

二、联盟成员讨论并通过《丝绸之路国际博物馆联盟章程》，同意遵守此章程文件，共同推进丝绸之路沿线国家和地区之间博物馆间的合作与交流。

三、联盟成员共同签署《丝绸之路国际博物馆联盟展览合作框架协议》，共同参与于 2019 年 3 月在中国国家博物馆举办的"文明的交流与互鉴"主题展览。

四、联盟门户网站正式上线，其运营由中国国家博物馆负责，网站将及时更新联盟发展动态信息，发布合作成果。

五、通过联盟成员讨论，联盟新增 4 家外国副理事长单位加入执行理事会。具体名单为：

1. 缅甸国家博物馆（仰光）

2. 哈萨克斯坦国家博物馆

3. 阿塞拜疆国家历史博物馆

4. 塞尔维亚国家博物馆

六、第二届丝绸之路国际博物馆联盟大会将于 2020 年 11 月在位于中国北京的中国国家博物馆举办。此后每两年召开的联盟大会由有能力举办的成员单位轮流主持，具体召开时间和议程由各成员单位协商，协商结果由联盟秘书处通知各成员。

联盟与会代表签字：

中国国家博物馆馆长　王春法

中国博物馆协会秘书长　安来顺

中国丝绸博物馆馆长　赵丰

福建博物院院长　吴志跃

西安大唐西市博物馆馆长　王彬

阿塞拜疆国家历史博物馆馆长　纳伊拉·瓦利克哈诺娃

哈萨克斯坦国家博物馆副馆长　萨图巴尔丁·阿拜·卡雷姆塔叶维奇

哈萨克斯坦中央国家博物馆考古中心负责人　哈米特·阿依特古

柬埔寨国家博物馆馆长　孔·维列

老挝国家博物馆馆长　佩玛莱婉·乔本玛

蒙古国国家博物馆政策规划和管理主管　布德巴亚尔·伊什根

缅甸国家博物馆（仰光）馆长　杜楠劳宁

Orit Shamir

以色列文物局博物馆及展览部主任奥丽特·沙米尔

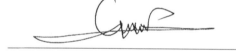

摩洛哥阿扎尔协会项目主管　奥马尔·伊德塔涅

白俄罗斯国家历史博物馆考古、钱币和兵器部主任　卢达·托尔卡切娃

俄罗斯斯塔夫罗波尔考古所　高级研究员　兹韦兹达娜·多德

塞尔维亚国家博物馆馆长　博亚娜·博里奇·布雷斯科维奇

2018 年 11 月 25 日
中国福州

成果文件 3:

丝绸之路国际博物馆联盟章程

一、总则

丝绸之路国际博物馆联盟（简称"联盟"），英文名称 International Alliance of Museums of the Silk Road（简称"IAMS"），是一个丝绸之路沿线国家和地区在博物馆领域的非政府性、非营利性的、开放的国际合作机制及交流平台。

联盟成员间应相互理解、相互尊重、相互信任。

二、宗旨

联盟将致力于积极探索在丝绸之路沿线国家和地区开展文化遗产领域的主题展览、信息共享、联合研究、专业人员交流和人才培养，推动沿线国家和地区之间的博物馆开展国际合作，并加强与各博物馆相关国际机构和组织之间的联系与合作，同时提高国际社会对跨文化交流合作的关注度和参与度，实现丝绸之路上的民心相通。

宗旨如下：

（一）通过实施与展览、专业人员和文物保护等博物馆相关业务的合作与交流，增进相互理解和友谊。

（二）通过开展数字化领域的合作，探讨丝绸之路沿线国家和地区博物馆联盟信息共享网站的可行性。

（三）通过定期联盟大会，向世界广泛传播丝绸之路沿线国家和地区丰富的历史和文化。

（四）鼓励联盟成员间进行以下方面的合作：

1. 定期举办丝绸之路国际博物馆联盟大会；

2. 配合联盟大会，举办联合展览；

3. 配合联盟大会，举办馆长论坛；

4. 开展联盟馆际间的展览交流活动；

5. 开展联盟馆际间专业人员交流与培训；

6. 开展联盟馆际间在文物保护领域的交流与合作；

7. 开展数字化领域的合作，探讨丝绸之路沿线国家和地区博物馆联盟信息共享网站的可行性；

8. 开展其他与博物馆相关的交流与合作。

三、成员

现有成员单位共计 157 个，其中国际机构 47 个，国内机构 110 个。

（一）成员申请及退出程序

联盟本着开放的精神，联盟成员将逐步壮大。会员入会程序如下：

1. 提交入会申请书；

2. 经执行理事会讨论通过；

3. 由秘书处发给会员证书。

成员单位退出联盟应书面通知秘书处，连续 5 年不参加联盟的活动，其成员资格将自动取消。

（二）成员申请资格

1. 拥护联盟成立倡议书和本章程；

2. 有加入联盟的意愿；

3. 在博物馆行业内具有一定的影响；

4. 服从联盟领导，积极参加联盟组织的各项活动。

（三）成员单位的权利

1. 按照本章程及相关协议，共享联盟资源；

2. 经执行理事会批准，可以联盟名义举办或承办活动；

3. 自愿加入、退出联盟。

（四）成员单位的义务

1. 遵守本章程和规章制度，执行联盟决议；

2. 积极参与联盟活动，提供资源支持，努力推动联盟的建设和发展；

3. 维护联盟的利益和合法权益；

4. 对以联盟名义组织申请或承担的项目，应接受联盟的监督和检查，并按照约定履行合同。

四、组织

组织机构由执行理事会、秘书处构成。

（一）执行理事会

由理事长、秘书长、副理事长组成，现有成员 10 人，成员总数应不超过 21 人。

1. 执行理事会成员如下：

（1）理事长 —— 中国国家博物馆馆长

（2）秘书长 —— 中国国家博物馆副馆长

（3）副理事长 —— 中国博物馆协会秘书长

（4）副理事长 —— 中国丝绸博物馆馆长

（5）副理事长 —— 福建博物院院长

（6）副理事长 —— 西安大唐西市博物馆馆长

（7）副理事长 —— 缅甸国家博物馆（仰光）馆长

（8）副理事长 —— 哈萨克斯坦国家博物馆馆长

（9）副理事长 —— 阿塞拜疆国家历史博物馆馆长

（10）副理事长 —— 塞尔维亚国家博物馆馆长

2. 任期

执行理事会成员因退休、离职等不再担任其所在单位职务，而由其他人员替代的，应及时将继任者名单通知秘书处，经执行理事会会议通过确认。

3.理事长权限

理事长有权召集执行理事会会议。

4.理事长责任

理事长有责任将执行理事会会议做出的决定通知各联盟成员。

5.秘书长职责

（1）管理秘书处日常工作，组织实施年度工作计划；

（2）处理其他日常事务。

（二）秘书处

秘书处设在中国国家博物馆（中国北京天安门广场东侧）

1.联盟秘书处办公室主任：中国国家博物馆外事部门负责人

2.联盟秘书处办公室副主任：中国博物馆协会副秘书长

3.联盟秘书处成员：中国国家博物馆工作人员

（三）联络官

每一联盟成员单位应设立联络办公室，并指定联络官负责与秘书处的联络工作。

五、会议

（一）联盟大会每两年举办一次。每次大会围绕一个主题，探讨促进丝绸之路沿线国家和地区博物馆发展与合作的有效路径，回应共同关切，共创美好未来。

（二）执行理事会议每年至少召开一次，秘书处召集，执行理事参与。执行理事成员数过半即可召开，其决议通过方能生效。

（三）首届联盟大会和执行理事会议于2018年11月在中国福建省召开，讨论并通过联盟章程。

六、经费

中国国家博物馆负责联盟秘书处日常开支，鼓励各联盟成员积极开展活动，具体活动经费由参与单位共同筹措。

七、争议解决方式

在发生争议时，应按照友好协商的原则处理；在协商无果的情况下，提交第三方仲裁机构仲裁，仲裁裁决为最终裁定，对争议各方都有约束力。

八、附则

（一）本章程于 2018 年 11 月 24 日召开的首届联盟大会上表决通过并即时生效。

（二）本章程的解释权和修订归执行理事会。

2018 年 11 月 24 日

成果文件 4：

丝绸之路国际博物馆联盟
展览合作框架协议

丝绸之路国际博物馆联盟（简称"联盟"），英文名称 International Alliance of Museums of the Silk Road（简称"IAMS"），是一个丝绸之路沿线国家和地区在博物馆领域的非政府性、非营利性的、开放的国际合作机制及交流平台。

为充分体现多样性和全球性，体现交流与合作，作为联盟的理事长单位，中国国家博物馆将联合全球 17 个国家级博物馆于 2019 年年初在北京举办"文明的交流与互鉴"主题展览。展览将通过文物来反映丝绸之路各国间在商贸往来、信仰传播、科学技术、生活方式、文化艺术等方面的交流历史，表现世界不同文明之间的对话与融合，从而为今天"一带一路"框架下各国家地区间实现文明交流互鉴、合作共赢提供历史借鉴。

值此丝绸之路国际博物馆首届联盟大会举行之际，在《丝绸之路国际博物馆联盟章程》框架下，我们，来自 12 个国家的 17 家单位，一致同意共同参与此"文明的交流与互鉴"主题展览，以实现和平合作、开放包容、互学互鉴、互利共赢为核心的丝路精神。

联盟与会代表签字：

中国国家博物馆馆长　王春法

中国博物馆协会秘书长　安来顺

中国丝绸博物馆馆长　赵丰

福建博物院院长　吴志跃

西安大唐西市博物馆馆长　王彬

阿塞拜疆国家历史博物馆馆长　纳伊拉·瓦利克哈诺娃

哈萨克斯坦国家博物馆副馆长　萨图巴尔丁·阿拜·卡雷姆塔叶维奇

哈萨克斯坦中央国家博物馆考古中心负责人　哈米特·阿依特古

柬埔寨国家博物馆馆长　孔·维列

老挝国家博物馆馆长　佩玛莱婉·乔本玛

蒙古国国家博物馆政策规划和管理主管　布德巴亚尔·伊什根

缅甸国家博物馆（仰光）馆长　杜楠劳宁

Orit Shamir

以色列文物局博物馆及展览部主任奥丽特·沙米尔

摩洛哥阿扎尔协会项目主管　奥马尔·伊德塔涅

白俄罗斯国家历史博物馆考古、钱币和兵器部主任　卢达·托尔卡切娃

俄罗斯斯塔夫罗波尔考古所　高级研究员　兹韦兹达娜·多德

塞尔维亚国家博物馆馆长　博亚娜·博里奇·布雷斯科维奇

2018 年 11 月 24 日
中国福州

附 录 ▪
Appendix

丝绸之路国际博物馆联盟成员名单

截至 2018 年 11 月，丝绸之路国际博物馆联盟成员单位共计 157 家，其中国际成员 47 家，中国成员 110 家。

国际成员

亚洲

阿塞拜疆国家历史博物馆

巴基斯坦国立自然历史博物馆

巴勒斯坦博物馆

哈萨克斯坦国家博物馆

哈萨克斯坦国立中央博物馆

韩国传统文化大学

吉尔吉斯斯坦国家历史博物馆

吉尔吉斯斯坦伏龙芝博物馆

柬埔寨国家博物馆

老挝国家博物馆

蒙古国国家博物馆

缅甸国家博物馆（仰光）

塔吉克斯坦国家博物馆

塔吉克斯坦库洛布博物馆群

泰国诗丽吉皇后纺织博物馆

乌兹别克斯坦国家历史博物馆

乌兹别克斯坦布哈拉博物馆

乌兹别克斯坦科学院考古研究所

也门国家博物馆

以色列国家文物局

印度世界文化研究所

印度尼西亚东南亚传统纺织品艺术联盟

非洲

阿尔及利亚麦迪亚博物馆

埃塞俄比亚国家博物馆

摩洛哥阿扎特协会

塞内加尔黑人文明博物馆

坦桑尼亚国家博物馆

欧洲

白俄罗斯国家历史博物馆

丹麦国家研究基金会纺织品研究中心

丹麦国家博物馆

德国马克思·普朗克科学史研究所

俄罗斯国家历史博物馆

俄罗斯国立艾尔米塔什博物馆

俄罗斯国立东方艺术博物馆

俄罗斯民族志博物馆

俄罗斯斯塔夫罗波尔考古所

俄罗斯北高加索地区古代史与考古研究所

法国纺织品艺术博物馆（里昂）

瑞典历史博物馆

塞尔维亚国家博物馆

乌克兰尼古拉巧克力博物馆

意大利帕多瓦大学

大英图书馆国际敦煌项目部

英国剑桥大学李约瑟研究所

英国剑桥大学麦克唐纳考古研究所

美洲

美国女神艺术博物馆

美国布莱恩特大学

中国成员

北京

中国国家博物馆

中国博物馆协会

故宫博物院

首都博物馆

北京大学中国古代史研究中心

中国海关博物馆

北京晋商博物馆

中国北京紫檀博物馆

中国科学院自然科学史研究所

天津

天津博物馆

天津沉香艺术博物馆

河北

河北博物院

河北大晟堂古陶博物馆

河北衡水内画艺术博物馆

孙瀛洲纪念馆

山西

大同市博物馆

临汾平阳木版年画博物馆

内蒙古

内蒙古博物院

呼和浩特市博物馆

内蒙古明博草原文化博物馆

辽宁

辽宁省博物馆

旅顺博物馆

吉林

吉林省博物院

黑龙江

黑龙江省博物馆

上海

上海博物馆

中国航海博物馆

上海世华艺术馆

上海琉璃艺术博物馆

东华大学服装与艺术设计学院

江苏

南京博物院

苏州博物馆

扬州博物馆

镇江博物馆

徐州圣旨博物馆

浙江

中国丝绸博物馆

浙江省博物馆

宁波博物院

浙江绍兴市越文化博物馆

浙江大学"一带一路"合作与发展协同创新中心

安徽

安徽博物院

安徽省源泉徽文化民俗博物馆

福建

福建博物院

福州市博物馆

泉州博物馆

陈嘉庚纪念馆

泉州海外交通史博物馆

福建省贞美历史文化博物馆

厦门奥林匹克博物馆

江西

江西省博物馆

山东

山东博物馆

青岛市博物馆

河南

河南博物院

洛阳博物馆

洛阳白河书斋晁氏藏书博物馆

郑州大象陶瓷博物馆

广东

广东省博物馆

广州博物馆

广东海上丝绸之路博物馆

广西

广西壮族自治区博物馆

海南

海南省博物馆

重庆

重庆中国三峡博物馆

重庆宝林博物馆

四川

四川博物院

成都博物馆

成都蜀锦织绣博物馆

四川建川博物馆

贵州

贵州省博物馆

云南

云南省博物馆

云南民族博物馆

西藏

西藏博物馆

陕西

西安大唐西市博物馆

陕西历史博物馆

陕西法门寺博物馆

西安博物院

陕西汉唐石刻博物馆

陕西万达博物院

陕西唐三彩艺术博物馆

西安关中民俗艺术博物院

西安市大唐青铜镜博物馆

西安唐皇城墙含光门遗址博物馆

西安源浩华藏博物馆

西安秦砖汉瓦博物馆

大明宫遗址博物馆

咸阳博物院

国际古迹遗址理事会西安国际保护中心

甘肃

甘肃省博物馆

甘肃省文物考古研究所

敦煌研究院

甘肃炳灵寺文物保护研究所

甘肃麦积山石窟艺术研究所

兰州市博物馆

武威市博物馆

张掖市文物局

张掖市甘州区博物馆

酒泉市博物馆

嘉峪关长城博物馆

敦煌市博物馆

阳关博物馆

天水市博物馆

平凉市博物馆

青海

青海省博物馆

宁夏

宁夏回族自治区博物馆

宁夏水洞沟遗址博物馆

宁夏固原博物馆

新疆

新疆维吾尔自治区博物馆

吐鲁番博物馆

伊犁哈萨克族自治州博物馆

新疆维吾尔自治区文物考古研究所

香港

香港明清家具馆

澳门

澳门中华艺术交流促进会

参会机构介绍

阿塞拜疆国家历史博物馆

阿塞拜疆国家历史博物馆成立于 1920 年 6 月 15 日，是阿塞拜疆第一座博物馆，同时也是科学教育中心。建馆以来，博物馆一直致力于不断丰富馆藏，收集与保护古今各类文物。目前藏品数量约 30 万件。博物馆设有 11 座藏品库房，考古学、民族志、钱币学等 6 个学术部门，还设有文物修复实验室和图书馆。

阿塞拜疆国家历史博物馆成立近百年来，一直以文化遗产保护为己任，已成为历史研究领域重要的学术及文化中心。博物馆亦是隶属于阿塞拜疆科学院的科学研究机构，出版发行普及性与学术性出版物，如各类画册、藏品目录、书籍和学术专著等。

　　阿塞拜疆国家历史博物馆与世界各地博物馆均有合作，包括中国、土耳其、俄罗斯、德国、格鲁吉亚、乌兹别克斯坦、哈萨克斯坦、意大利、法国和波兰等国家。博物馆还积极参与文化遗产领域的各类学术会议、专题研讨、论坛，促进信息共享，开展联合研究，举办文化遗产类专业交流及人才培训。阿塞拜疆国家历史博物馆曾在德国、英国、挪威、梵蒂冈、捷克和哈萨克斯坦等国举办展览。

　　每天都有大量观众前来博物馆参观，博物馆团队也在努力吸引更多游客并使之了解阿塞拜疆丰富的文化和历史。

哈萨克斯坦国家博物馆

　　哈萨克斯坦国家博物馆是哈萨克斯坦国家历史的珍贵组成部分，是哈萨克斯坦民族文化不可分割的一部分，是具有国家意义的重要项目。哈萨克斯坦国家博物馆根据哈萨克斯坦共和国总统努尔苏丹·纳扎尔巴耶夫的命令于 2014 年 7 月 2 日成立。博物馆有 10 个常设展厅，展览空间逾 1.4 万平方米，建筑总面积 7.4 万平方米，位列世界十大博物馆之一，是中亚最大的博物馆。博物馆中庭凭借卓越的声光融合效果吸引着众多游客。展览和永久陈列介绍了哈萨克斯坦从古至今的历史与文化。

　　哈萨克斯坦国家博物馆的主建筑和谐地融入阿斯塔纳的天际线和独立广场周边的建筑群落，与哈萨克民族纪念碑、独立宫、和平金字塔、国立艺术大学以及哈兹拉特苏丹清真寺共同组成亮丽的风景。

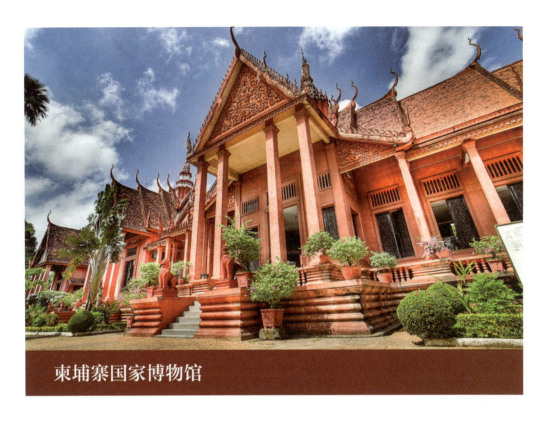

柬埔寨国家博物馆

　　柬埔寨国家博物馆位于柬埔寨首都金边，是该国首屈一指的历史学和考古学博物馆。博物馆始建于 1917 年至 1920 年，是世界上收藏高棉物质文化遗产最为丰富的博物馆之一，主要致力于柬埔寨文化和艺术遗产的保护、收藏、宣传、修复以及传承，通过展览馆内的展览，让观众能够直观理解并感受柬埔寨的文化遗产。

　　柬埔寨国家博物馆总面积约 5200 平方米，其中展览面积 2800 平方米。博物馆建筑采用人字屋顶和雕花大门、高棉古寺建筑样式，融高棉传统建筑与法国殖民风格为一体，是金边市经典建筑之一。

　　目前，博物馆藏品共计约 15,000 件，每期固定陈列展出约 2000 件。馆内藏品丰富，跨越不同历史时期——既包括史前阶段，也包括前吴哥时期、吴哥时期、后吴哥时期等不同阶段的文物。这些藏品主要有四类：石器、青铜器、瓷器以及木器。石器主要是婆罗门教和佛教传说中神的石雕作品，其中碑刻和建筑样式颇具代表性。馆内收藏的青铜器多为宗教人物雕像以及日常生活中用的礼器和生活用具。藏品中还有一些陶器、瓷器和兽型容器等反映人类文明的文物。木器多为讲经布道用的长椅，及箱子、盘子、织机和其他雕刻物。此外，博物馆还收藏有少量油画、纺织品、图片及其他档案资料。

老挝国家博物馆

老挝国家博物馆是科学研究中心，也是致力于研究、保护、促进老挝文化和历史的公共机构。博物馆老馆所在建筑始建于1925年，是老挝仍在使用的最古老的殖民建筑之一。1985年博物馆被命名为老挝革命博物馆，2000年改名为老挝国家博物馆。2017年博物馆新馆建成启用。馆内藏品包含28,000余件已登记文物和约130,000件尚未登记的文物。自2000年以来，老挝国家博物馆每年接待数以千计的海内外游客和学生。

缅甸国家博物馆（仰光）

　　缅甸国家博物馆（仰光）于 1952 年缅甸独立时由缅甸文化部建立。博物馆展品最初曾存放在朱比莉宫，1970 年迁至潘索丹路，1996 年 9 月 18 日迁至现在的仰光大衮乡卑谬路 66/47 号。博物馆坐落在一座宏伟的五层建筑内，展厅面积达1.8 万平方米。

　　缅甸国家博物馆（仰光）以收集、保护并展示缅甸文化遗产为己任，致力于成为公众了解缅甸文化及文明进程的中心，通过保护缅甸的文化遗产以塑造更美好的未来。基于这一愿景，博物馆将多种主题的展览融为一体，包括历史、考古、艺术与手工艺、民族学等。博物馆拥有 13 个展厅，共展出超过 4000 件藏品，其中最古老的藏品有四千万年历史，早于人类的进化史。

　　缅甸国家博物馆（仰光）现有收藏、博物馆财产的保存与保护、研究与出版、展览（常设展与临时展）、公共教育等五项职能。

以色列文物局

以色列文物局是负责保护国家文物和古迹的独立政府机构，依照 1978 年的《文物法》开展对本国文物和古迹的发掘、保存、保护、研究和出版工作，并力图在国家发展需求和文物保护之间保持平衡。

以色列文物局每年开展约 150 次抢救性发掘，出土大量历史文物。该局负责监督考古陈列并协助其升级维护，以提高公众对国家考古遗产的保护意识和兴趣。

以色列有约 350 个考古博物馆、展览及户外展陈遍布全国各地，其中一些拥有数十年历史。自 1948 年以色列建国以来，考古博物馆和展览一直广受欢迎。公众对考古学的兴趣使得大规模收藏兴起，其中一些藏品得以在博物馆展出。按规定，博物馆收藏和展览展出的所有考古文物均须在以色列文物局登记。

以色列文物局还负责管理和出借考古文物，鼓励在各地博物馆、国立机构、公共机构、研究和教育机构、国家公园、游客中心和学校等各类场所举办展览。

白俄罗斯国家历史博物馆

　　白俄罗斯国家历史博物馆起源于一家 1919 年成立的地方性历史博物馆，2009 年更名为白俄罗斯国家历史博物馆。博物馆现有五个分馆：俄国社会民主工党一大会址纪念馆、白俄罗斯戏剧音乐文化历史博物馆、白俄罗斯电影历史博物馆、现代白俄罗斯国家制度博物馆、白俄罗斯自然生态博物馆。白俄罗斯国家历史博物馆现有藏品 46 万余件（套）。很多珍贵藏品被列入白俄罗斯国家历史文化遗产名录，包括罗马银币（公元 1 至 2 世纪）、银腰带套组（14 世纪末至 15 世纪初）、圣门（18 世纪）和佚名艺术家创作的约瑟夫·普罗佐肖像画（18 世纪末至 19 世纪初）。博物馆与私人藏家合作密切。2008 年，以博物馆为基础，成立了白俄罗斯国家博物馆馆藏目录中心，收集白俄罗斯各博物馆中最具价值的藏品的信息。

　　白俄罗斯国家博物馆有很多科技创新，包括弗朗西斯克·斯卡伊那生平和著作的多媒体展示，结合创新科技制作的弗朗西斯克·斯卡伊那圣经的高清版本，可佩戴增强现实眼镜观看的三维 Kreva 城堡和 Halshany 城堡模型等。

俄罗斯斯塔夫罗波尔考古所

俄罗斯斯塔夫罗波尔考古所成立于 1995 年。研究所的工作包括历史文化古迹的考古研究、开发建设区域内的历史文化古迹的认定、文物和考古纺织品的保护、考古研究地理信息技术的开发与部署等。同时，研究所参与了一系列内容广泛的国际合作，从联合考古发掘到古欧亚大陆人口基因组研究等领域均有涉及。

塞尔维亚国家博物馆

塞尔维亚国家博物馆是一家综合博物馆，是塞尔维亚最大、历史最为悠久的中央博物馆。博物馆自 1844 年成立以来，现有 34 个藏品门类，藏品逾 45 万件，是塞尔维亚、巴尔干半岛中部和欧洲独特文化遗产的集大成者。

塞尔维亚国家博物馆致力于保护、阐释和宣传塞尔维亚及本地区多层次的文化遗产，是知识的源泉，也是活跃的社区学习中心。塞尔维亚国家博物馆曾经是，未来也将继续成为巴尔干地区最重要的博物馆学中心，以及具有当地和世界影响力的国家文化中心。

中国国家博物馆

　　中国国家博物馆是代表国家征集、收藏、保管、展示、阐释能够充分反映中华优秀传统文化、革命文化和社会主义先进文化代表性物证的最高机构，是国家最高历史文化艺术殿堂和文化客厅。2012 年 11 月 29 日，习近平总书记率领十八届中央政治局常委来到中国国家博物馆参观"复兴之路"基本陈列，发出实现中华民族伟大复兴中国梦的伟大号召，中国特色社会主义新时代在这里扬帆启程。

　　中国国家博物馆现有藏品数量 140 余万件，涵盖古代文物、近现代文物、图书古籍善本、艺术品等多种门类。拥有展厅 48 个，建筑面积近 20 万平方米，是世界上单体建筑面积最大的博物馆。展览包括基本陈列、专题展览、临时展览三大系列，构成涵盖基本陈列、专题陈列、重大主题展览、精品文物展、考古发现展、经典美术作品展、地域文化展和国际交流展的展览体系。2018 年国家博物馆观众人数达 861 余万人，创造观众参观历史新高，是世界上最受欢迎的博物馆之一。

中国丝绸博物馆

中国丝绸博物馆于 1992 年正式对外开放，2016 年经全面改扩建后重新启用。中国丝绸博物馆是一个以中国丝绸为核心的，集纺织服装文化遗产收藏、保护、研究、展示、传承和创新于一体的国家一级博物馆。目前占地 4 万平方米，陈列面积 1 万平方米，设有丝路馆、蚕桑馆、织造馆、纺织品文物修复展示馆、时装馆、新猷资料馆和女红传习馆。馆内还有锦绣廊、经纶堂丝绸精品店、丝博商场，可供品尝咖啡，阅览图书，购买丝绸相关的文创产品及丝绸制品。

福建博物院

福建博物院于 1933 年成立，2002 年重建于西湖之畔，是首批国家一级博物馆，是全国范围内唯一集博物馆、自然馆、积翠园艺术馆、考古研究所、文物保护中心、国家水下考古基地"六合一"的综合性博物馆。拥有馆藏文物和各类标本 28 万余件，其中珍贵文物 3 万余件。除设立"福建古代文明之光""弦歌悠远""意匠天工""闽迹寻踪""丝路帆远""恐龙世界""闽海蔚蓝"等基本陈列外，每年还举办 30 多个临时展览。

福建博物院在策划展览、服务品牌、学术研究、管理模式上突破创新，取得显著成果：2015 年获"全国最具创新力博物馆"称号，成为本次唯一获此殊荣的国有博物馆。2016 年获由国际博物馆协会基金会等组织颁发的"2016 年度全球博物馆及文化遗产保护领域最杰出、最具创新力、最具合作启发意义项目"奖，并获邀加入"最佳文化遗产组织杰出俱乐部"。福建博物院是全球唯一一家参加维也纳联合国总部研讨会的博物馆，院长吴志跃在研讨会上发表"丝路帆远行万里"的主旨演讲。

西安大唐西市博物馆

　　西安大唐西市博物馆是建于丝绸之路东方起点唐长安城西市遗址之上，以反映丝绸之路文化和商业文化为主题的中国首座民营遗址类博物馆，馆藏文物两万余件，上起商周，下迄明清，跨越绵绵三千余载。精美神秘的青铜器、绚丽多彩的陶瓷器、千姿百态的陶俑、璀璨夺目的金银器、精美绝伦的丝绸、巧夺天工的玉器，还有大量的货币、墓志、宗教、建筑类文物充盈库藏，为精彩纷呈的陈列展览奠定了坚实基础。目前是中国首家也是唯一一家非国有国家一级博物馆。

Overview ■
综述

Overview of the First Conference of the International Alliance of Museums of the Silk Road

In order to implement the spirit of President Xi Jinping's important speeches on the Silk Road Economic Belt and the 21st Century Maritime Silk Road, strengthen the mutual learning of civilizations and people-to-people connections with countries and regions along the Belt and Road, and effectively promote the innovative development of cultural exchanges, communication and trade, the First Conference of the International Alliance of Museums of the Silk Road was successfully held in Fuzhou, Fujian Province, China, from November 24 to 25, 2018. Dr. Wang Chunfa, Director of the National Museum of China delivered a welcome speech. Mr. Guan Qiang, Deputy Administrator of the National Cultural Heritage Administration of China, Mr. Zhu Qi, Deputy Director of Bureau of International Exchange and Cooperation, Ministry of Culture and Tourism of China, and Ms. Li Chun, Deputy Mayor of the People's Government of Fuzhou Municipality, delivered speeches at the opening ceremony. Representatives from more than 30 cultural institutions of over 20 countries, including the National Museum of History of Azerbaijan, the National Museum of Cambodia, the National Museum of the Republic of Kazakhstan, the Lao National Museum, the National Museum of Myanmar (Yangon), the National Museum in Belgrade, Republic of Serbia, the National Museum of Mongolia, and the National Historical Museum of the Republic of Belarus attended the conference. The conference achieved important outcomes and received positive responses from the participants and the media.

I. Origin of the First Conference of the International Alliance of Museums of the Silk Road

When visiting Kazakhstan and Indonesia in September and October of 2013, Chinese President Xi Jinping raised the initiative of jointly building the Silk Road Economic Belt and the 21st Century Maritime Silk Road (hereinafter referred to as the Belt and Road Initiative), which has drawn wide attention of the world. In order to promote the implementation of the Belt and Road Initiative, to revitalize the ancient Silk Road, to bring Asian, European and African countries closer together in a new form, and to achieve even greater development in mutually beneficial cooperation, the Chinese government published the Vision and Actions on Jointly Building Silk Road Economic Belt and 21st Century Maritime Silk Road in March 2015. On December 29, 2016, the former Ministry of Culture of China (now Ministry of Culture and Tourism of China) issued Ministry of Culture Belt and Road Cultural Development Action Plan (2016-2020), one important goal of which is to improve the Belt and Road cultural exchange and cooperation mechanism. The plan proposes to establish five alliances to lead the mechanism construction, including the International Alliance of Museums of the Silk Road, the Silk Road International League of Theatres, the Silk Road International Library Alliance, the Silk Road International Alliance of Art Museums, and the Network of Silk Road Arts Festivals.

In this context,on May 18, 2017, three organizations including the Committee of Museums Along the Silk Road of Chinese Museums Association, the International Association for the Study of Silk Roads Textiles (IASSRT), and the Silk Road International Museum Alliance with 145 museums and institutions (including 37 international institutions and 108 Chinese institutions) from Asia, Africa, Europe and America together proposed the establishment of the International Alliance of Museums of the Silk Road (hereinafter referred to as the IAMS). Witnessed by then China's Minister of Culture Mr. Luo Shugang, Administrator of the National Cultural Heritage Administration of China Mr. Liu Yuzhu, and Deputy Administrator of the National Cultural Heritage Administration of China Mr. Guan Qiang, the International Alliance of Museums of the Silk Road Initiative was signed by Director of the Central State Museum of Kazakhstan Mr. Nursan Alimbay, Director of the Pakistan Museum of Natural History Mr. Muhammad Akhter Javed, Director of National Museum of Tanzania Mr. Audax ZP Mabulla, along with the Committee of Museums Along the Silk Road of Chinese Museums Association, the International Association for the Study of Silk Roads Textiles (IASSRT) and the Silk Road International Museum Alliance.

On June 29, 2018, the leading Party members group of the Ministry of Culture and Tourism of China decided to relocate the Secretariat of the International Alliance of Museums of the Silk Road to the National Museum of China. The National Museum of China henceforth acted as the lead unit of the alliance, and Director Wang Chunfa became the alliance president.

On July 6, 2018, according to the spirit of President Xi Jinping's instruction and the work arrangements of the Ministry of Culture and Tourism's Belt and Road Cultural Development Action Plan, the IAMS first working meeting was held at the National Museum of China after the relocation of the Secretariat. After discussion, four initiating institutions, the Chinese Museums Association, the China National Silk Museum, the Fujian Museum and the Xi'an Tang West Market Museum were confirmed as Vice President units, and the meeting decided to prepare for the first Conference of the IAMS. After preparation over four months, to actively fulfill duties and obligations, the National Museum of China took the lead in convening alliance members to hold the first conference in Fuzhou, an important starting point for the ancient Maritime Silk Road, from November 24 to 25, 2018. The conference is dedicated to exploring the development of themed exhibitions, information sharing, joint research, personnel exchanges, and training in the field of cultural heritage in countries and regions along the Silk Road. It plays an important role in promoting international cooperation among museums along the Silk Road.

II. Convening the IAMS First Conference to promote the alliance's institutional development and explore opportunities for cooperation on the theme of the Silk Road

Fourteen representatives of Chinese and international members introduced their institutions and expressed their willing to support the Belt and Road Initiative under the frame of the IAMS, and therefore to advance practical cooperation and practice the Silk Road Spirit featuring peace and cooperation, openness and inclusiveness and mutual learning and mutual benefit, to embrace the opportunities and challenges brought by the in-depth development of the world's multi-polarization, economic globalization, social informatization and cultural diversity.

Dr. Wang Chunfa, President of the IAMS and Director of the National Museum of China, stated in his welcome speech that museums have a unique function of cultural interaction. The establishment and development of the IAMS demonstrates the awareness of "a community of shared future" that features unity in times of difficulty and the sharing of rights and obligations. By taking action to strengthen cooperation and revitalize museum collections, alliance members enhance mutual learning and achieve mutual benefit while respecting diversity of civilizations, paths and differences in unbalanced development. He suggested that through joint contribution, shared benefits and win-win cooperation, all members shall bring more benefits to peoples of countries along the Silk Road and build a global community of shared future. As the President unit of the IAMS, the National Museum of China will actively fulfill its duties and obligations, function as a bridge and bond, establish and improve a communication mechanism, create a cooperation platform, and provide necessary services to ensure effective operation of the IAMS.

Officials from the National Cultural Heritage Administration of China, the Bureau of International Exchange and Cooperation, Ministry of Culture and Tourism of China, and the People's Government of Fuzhou Municipality attended the conference and delivered speeches.

Mr. Guan Qiang, Deputy Administrator of the National Cultural Heritage Administration of China, welcomed all representatives and guests, and expressed his heartfelt congratulations on the convening of the conference at the opening ceremony. He stated that the Silk Road has always been the most important trade route and cultural link between the East and the West in the ancient world. Today, the Silk Road is more than a route. In recent years, a number of cooperation projects were made between China and countries along the Silk Road and international organizations, which reflects that the Chinese government gives high priority over the protection of cultural heritage along the Silk Road and proactively shoulders the responsibility for cultural heritage protection. He hopes that on the IAMS platform, members will continue close cooperation, complement each others' strengths, achieve common progress, and explore new ways for mutual learning among Silk Road civilizations.

Mr. Zhu Qi, Deputy Director of Bureau of International Exchange and Cooperation, Ministry of Culture and Tourism of China, expressed his expectations for the conference. He hopes that the conference will provide new opportunities for museums to share resources, exchange experiences, pool wisdom, and seek common development, and countries along the Silk Road will continue to promote cultural exchanges and cooperation in a close, positive and friendly direction, to further enhance the international influence and appeal of building the Belt and Road and attract more and more countries along the Belt and Road to join in.

Ms. Li Chun, Deputy Mayor of the People's Government of Fuzhou, introduced in her remarks that Fuzhou was an important starting point for the ancient Maritime Silk Road. She hopes that the conference participants' insightful new ideas will help promote the cultural and museum development in Fuzhou.

Ms. Bojana Borić-Brešković, Director of the National Museum in Belgrade, Republic of Serbia, said museum exhibitions should be educational and entertaining at the same time. In her view, the criterion for the success of a museum exhibition should be whether it offers visitors emotional experience, rather than having visitors leaving the museum merely learning specific facts or scientific principles.

Mr. Zhao Feng, Director of China National Silk Museum, shared the museum's successful experience in scientific research, identification, protection and conservation of textile relics, and introduced an exhibition the museum was organizing, namely *Life along the Silk Road: 13 Stories*

during the Great Era. He invites all members to participate in the project "Interactive World Map of Silk", which aims to carry out comprehensive and systematic survey of textile resources along the Silk Road and to have these resources digitalized and archived, so as to lay a solid foundation for international study on Silk Roads textiles. He also recommends the alliance to set up special committees to lead works in areas such as exhibitions, conservation and training.

Mr. Wu Zhiyue, Director of the Fujian Museum, introduced the museum's rich collection of Maritime Silk Road, shared their successful experience in curating joint exhibitions of Maritime Silk Road cultural relics and academic studies in the fields related to the Silk Road, and new findings in underwater cultural heritage protection projects.

Ms. Wang Bin, Director of Xi'an Tang West Market Museum, gave a detailed introduction of the museum's philosophy of development, features of collections, and exhibitions and activities themed on the Silk Road. She said the museum would continue to feature the culture of the Silk Road and promote cooperation with museums along the Silk Road to enlarge the circle of friends.

Mr. Huang Zhenchun, then Deputy Director of the National Museum of China, shared the museum's future plan of developing main and branch construction, promoting the development of Smart NMC, strengthening means of innovative dissemination, implementing the curator-centered exhibition system, and promoting inter-museum cooperation. He hopes to increase exhibition cooperation, promote exchanges and training events, and implement joint publishing with alliance members.

III. The conference was fruitful, and the future work of the IAMS was clarified

After two days of communication and discussion, with the extensive participation and joint efforts of representatives of the IAMS members, the conference achieved fruitful results.

First, member representatives discussed and adopted the Statutes of the International Alliance of Museums of the Silk Road, which defines the alliance's mission of actively exploring thematic exhibitions, information sharing, joint research, professional exchanges and personnel training in the field of cultural heritage in countries and regions along the Silk Road, promoting international cooperation among museums in countries and regions along the Silk Road, strengthening contact and cooperation with international institutions and organizations related to these museums, and improving the society's attention to and participation in cross-cultural exchanges and cooperation, thus forging a bond of friendships for all peoples on the Silk Road. It also stipulates the membership application and withdrawal procedures, and clarifies that the organization consists of the Executive Council and the Secretariat.

Second, the Framework Agreement on IAMS Exhibition Cooperation was fully discussed and signed by representatives of the IAMS members. The National Museum of China will partner with 17 national museums from 12 countries to host an exhibition in Beijing at the beginning of 2019 on the theme of "Exchanges and Mutual Learning among Civilizations". At the same time, the Global Museum Directors Forum will be held themed on "The Functions and Missions of National Museums along the Silk Road".

Third, the first meeting of the Executive Council of the IAMS was held. After discussion among members, it was agreed that four new international Vice-President units – National Museum of Myanmar (Yangon), National Museum of the Republic of Kazakhstan, National Museum of History of Azerbaijan and National Museum in Belgrade, Serbia will join the Executive Council.

Fourth, the IAMS website (www.musesilkroad.com) was officially launched, which was expected to strengthen the information exchange and resource sharing among member institutions, and to provide services and convenience for the cooperation and communication of museums and cultural protection institutions around the world.

Fifth, the conference participants jointly signed the Memorandum on the IAMS First Conference, and confirmed that the IAMS Conference would be held every two years.

Sixth, the future work of the IAMS was planned as follows:

A. To promote exhibition cooperation and advance exchanges and mutual learning among civilizations. Members of the IAMS shall launch at least one joint exhibition or tour exhibition each year.

B. To strengthen personnel exchanges and build synergies. All members shall take advantage of the IAMS platform to jointly develop professional talent training and academic exchanges in the fields of management, exhibition, archaeology, heritage conservation and research, and achieve normalization and institutionalization of professionals' exchange visits.

C. To carry out conservation of cultural relics and archaeological cooperation and jointly protect human cultural heritage. IAMS members should work together to explore a joint mechanism for scientific excavation, conservation and restoration of cultural relics, especially the exchanges and mutual learning of cultural relics conservation technologies in certain areas; to improve professional skills and operational ability and strengthen scientific excavation and preventive conservation of cultural relics; to jointly combat the smuggling and illegal trafficking of antiques in order to protect the cultural heritage shared by all mankind.

D. To promote the application of new technologies and the construction of smart museums and share innovative development experience. Museums and cultural institutions should take full advantage of the IAMS website to strengthen the digitization and informatization of member museums' collections, unblock the channels for resource sharing and information release and propel the sustainable and high-quality development of all members.

E. To strengthen the cooperation on cultural and creative development, bring cultural relics to life and realize the functional transformation of cultural relics. Alliance members shall rely on their featured collections to strengthen cooperation on IP authorization, joint research and development of cultural and creative products and give priority to alliance members for authorization, promotion and sales to enhance the cultural significance and intellectual value of cultural heritages.

For thousands of years, the Silk Road Spirit – "peace and cooperation, openness and inclusiveness, mutual learning and mutual benefit" – has been passed from generation to generation, promoted the progress of human civilization, and contributed greatly to the prosperity and development of the countries along the Silk Road. Symbolizing communication and cooperation between the East and the West, the Silk Road Spirit is a historic and cultural heritage shared by all countries around the world. In the 21st century, a new era marked by the theme of peace, development, cooperation and mutual benefit, it is all the more important for us to carry on the Silk Road Spirit in the face of the weak recovery of the global economy and complex international and regional situations.

Museums are sanctuaries that serves to protect and impart the fruits of civilization – bridges connecting the past, the present and the future. They play a special role in promoting exchanges and mutual learning between world civilizations. President of the IAMS Dr. Wang Chunfa proposes to continuously strengthen the mechanisms, clarify the goals and solidify the foundation for cooperation. At the same time, we should be aware of the importance of actively adapting to the new situation and changes, accelerating reform and innovation, stimulating the vitality of the museums' sustainable development, thereby bringing Asian, European and African countries closer together in a new form, and achieving even greater development in mutually beneficial cooperation. In the new era, at a new start and with a new mission, all the participating members agree to undertake responsibilities bravely, move forward unswervingly, take concrete actions to promote continuous new progress in the alliance work and inject strong impetus into building a human community with a shared future.

International Department
National Museum of China

Welcome Speech ■

欢迎致辞

Welcome Speech at the First Conference of the International Alliance of Museums of the Silk Road

Wang Chunfa
President, International Alliance of Museums of the Silk Road
Director, National Museum of China

It is my great honor to greet you in Fuzhou on the occasion of the convening of the First Conference of the International Alliance of Museums of the Silk Road.

The ancient Song dynasty ship excavated in Quanzhou, Fujian province is the earliest

wooden seacraft in the world. It bears witness to the great Chinese endeavor on the sea. The Chinese ancestors braved the terrible sea waves and explored a maritime Silk Road that connected East and West. Fujian as one of the starting points of the Maritime Silk Road is an important window to the world.

In 2013, Chinese President Xi Jinping proposed the Belt and Road Initiative that combined the Chinese Dream and dreams of countries along the Belt and Road and enriched the ancient Silk Road with brand-new implications. The Silk Road Spirit, with "peace and cooperation, openness and mutual accommodation, mutual learning and mutual benefit" as the cores, opens a new window for friendly exchanges among countries and a new chapter of progress of humanity.

Growing multipolarity, economic globalization, social informationization, and cultural diversity have brought both opportunities and challenges. Global economic growth, inclusive and balanced development, filling the great gap between the rich and the poor, and so on are problems that we need to face together and think about.

Cultural exchange contributes to the world cultural prosperity and world peace. Museum as an important place of protecting and inheriting human civilization plays a special role in promoting exchanges and mutual learning among world civilizations.

On May 18, 2017, under the auspices of the National Cultural Heritage Administration of China, the International Alliance of Museums of the Silk Road (IAMS) was established, uniting 145 Chinese and foreign cultural institutions. The IAMS aims at themed exhibitions, information sharing, joint research, personnel exchange, and training in the field of cultural heritage in countries and regions along the Silk Road. At the IAMS First Conference, we are going to discuss and pass the IAMS Statutes, Framework Agreement on Exhibition Cooperation, and four Vice-President member units, sign the conference memorandum, and explore future plans for cooperation.

Today, representatives from cultural institutions around the world are gathering here to discuss plans for museum development in a new era. The IAMS First Conference has significance for museum to play its unique role of connecting cultures:

First, museum promotes peace and cooperation. The Silk Road witnesses kindness and friendliness of peoples in countries alongside, links East and West, and is a bridge of peace. The development of the IAMS complies with the internal requirements for the reform of global governance system and demonstrates the awareness of a "community of shared future" that features unity in times of difficulty and the sharing of rights and obligations.

Second, museum embraces openness and mutual accommodation. Civilization develops in openness, and peoples coexist in interaction. Different histories, national conditions, ethnic groups, and customs have given birth to diversified civilizations and have made the world colorful. We should ensure that when it comes to different civilizations, exchange will replace estrangement, mutual learning will replace clashes, and coexistence will replace a sense of superiority.

Third, museum encourages mutual learning. The Silk Road is more than a trade route. It spreads knowledge and facilitates exchanges. We should learn from each other and make progress together while respecting diversity of civilizations and paths and differences in unbalanced development.

Fourth, museum brings mutual benefit. The Silk Road witnessed the bustling scenes of visits and trade over land and brought progress and prosperity in countries and regions alongside. We should take action, strengthen cooperation, revitalize museum collections, and achieve mutual benefits.

The International Alliance of Museums of the Silk Road offers new thoughts and new plans for promoting exchanges and mutual learning among civilizations and strengthening the people-to-people bond. Through joint contribution, shared benefits, and win-win cooperation, we should bring more benefits to peoples of countries along the Silk Road and build a global community of shared future.

The National Museum of China as a member unit of the IAMS will actively fulfill its duties and obligations, function as a bridge and bond, establish and improve a communication mechanism, create a cooperation platform, and provide necessary services to ensure the IAMS work is well done.

The convening of the IAMS First Conference signals a great step forward of the IAMS development. Let's move hand in hand, work together, and look forward to fruitful achievements of cooperation between museums of the Silk Road.

I wish the conference every success. Have a wonderful time in Fuzhou!

Opening Speeches
开幕致辞

Opening Speech at the First Conference of the International Alliance of Museums of the Silk Road

Guan Qiang
Deputy Administrator, National Cultural Heritage Administration, China

On behalf of the National Cultural Heritage Administration of China, I warmly welcome all the guests attending the First Conference of the International Alliance of Museums of the Silk Road. Congratulations on the opening of the conference!

The Silk Road originated in ancient China and connected Asia, Africa, and Europe. It is an important passage for ancient trade and a bridge for communication among civilizations. The exquisite Chinese embroidery, which was found in ancient nomadic tombs of the Altay Mountains in the mid 20th century by former Soviet Union archaeologists, closely resembles silk fabrics from the Chu state tombs in Changsha, China's Hunan Province in terms of both pattern and technique. This fact indicates that as early as the 5th century BC, silk had already begun its travel from China to other parts of the world. During the Western Han dynasty, a traffic network was built up between China's Central Plains and Central Asia, West Asia, and Europe. The silk trade route across Eurasia flourished during the Han, Wei, Sui, and Tang periods and became the most important trade route and cultural link between East and West in the ancient world. Today, the Silk Road is more than a route. The initiative of jointly building the Silk Road Economic Belt and the 21st Century Maritime Silk Road raised by Chinese President Xi Jinping has received great international attention and is positively responded by many countries. This initiative has enormous significance for accelerating China's opening-up and promoting regional and global peace and development.

The Chinese government gives high priority over the protection of cultural heritage along the Silk Road. Some related sites have already been included in the World Heritage List. Cooperation mechanism between China and countries along the Silk Road and international organizations such as Silk Road heritage sites protection and museums alliance has been established. Joint archaeological survey is carried out with Kenya, Saudi Arabia, India, Bangladesh, and Uzbekistan. Major joint exhibitions have been launched in China and abroad on the Silk Road, Maritime Silk Road, Ancient Tea-Horse Road, and Northern Grassland Silk Road, etc. For a long time, China has been participating in cultural heritage protection and aid projects in countries along the Silk Road. In addition, China shoulders the international responsibility of cultural heritage protection through the ICOM International Training Centre for Museum Studies (ICOM-ITC) at the Palace Museum in Beijing, which has organized training courses on cultural heritage protection for museum professionals from ASEAN and African countries.

Strengthening international exchanges and cooperation in the museum sector is a responsibility and aspiration shared by countries along the Silk Road and international organizations. Under the auspices of the Chinese Ministry of Culture (now Ministry of Culture and Tourism) and the National Cultural Heritage Administration, around the International Museum Day on May 18, 2017, the International Alliance of Museums of the Silk Road (IAMS) was initiated and established by the Chinese Museums Association (CMA) on the basis of three organizations, namely the Special Committee of Museums of the Silk Road under the CMA, the International Friendly Alliance of Museums of the Silk Road, and the International Association for the Study of Silk Roads Textiles. The National Museum of China is responsible for the liaison of IAMS matters. We hope that on the current platform, the IAMS members will continue close cooperation, complement each other's strengths, achieve common progress, and explore new ways for mutual learning among Silk Road civilizations. We hope the IAMS members will carry out practical exchanges and cooperation and make more achievements in exhibitions, collection management, academic studies, training, joint archaeology, public education, public service, cultural industry development, etc. The National Cultural Heritage Administration and the Chinese Museums Association will give support and assistance to all these cooperative projects.

Today, with the opening of the IAMS First Conference, which is initiated by the National Museum of China, we are looking forward to a new era for the cooperation among museums of countries along the Belt and Road and new inspirations from members of the IAMS. I wish this conference a great success!

Opening Speech at the First Conference of the International Alliance of Museums of the Silk Road

Zhu Qi

Deputy Director, Bureau of International Exchange and Cooperation, Ministry of Culture and Tourism, China

It is a great pleasure to meet with you all in Fuzhou and to participate in the First Conference of the International Alliance of Museums of the Silk Road. On behalf of the Ministry of Culture and Tourism of the People's Republic of China, I would like to extend our warm congratulations on the convening of this conference!

The Land Silk Road is a land route that started from Xi'an and connected the Mediterranean countries through Central and West Asia. The Maritime Silk Road was formed during the Qin and Han dynasties and flourished during the Tang and Song dynasties. It was the earliest maritime route between China and foreign countries in ancient times. The ancient Silk Road was not only a route of trade and barter, but also a road of knowledge exchange. In the course of historical development, along the ancient Silk Road, Chinese and Western cultures met, exchanged, integrated, and constantly inspired new sparks, writing in the history of civilization a glorious chapter of "envoys and messengers greeting each other and merchants travelling on the road".

In September and October 2013, during his visits to Kazakhstan and Indonesia respectively, President Xi Jinping proposed to jointly build the Silk Road Economic Belt and the 21st Century Maritime Silk Road, major initiatives that aimed at jointly building a community with shared interests, future, and responsibility featuring political trust, economic integration, and cultural inclusiveness. Our revisiting of the Silk Road, adherence to win-win cooperation, and advocating of exchange and mutual learning are not only because of the growing awareness of the importance of global cooperation among peoples of the world, but also because of the world's wide recognition of the role of the Silk Road in history. From 2013 to the present, the Belt and Road Initiative, which borrows the historical symbol of the ancient Silk Road and holds high the banner of peace and development, has transformed ideas into action, vision into reality and has been widely welcomed and echoed around the world.

Since ancient times, Fujian has been one of the areas in the southeast coastal region of China with the most frequent economic and cultural exchanges with overseas countries. As an important freight port, Fujian is recognized by the world as the starting point of the Maritime Silk Road. It is of great significance that we are holding the First Conference of the International Alliance of Museums of the Silk Road here today. On May 18, 2017, in order to comprehensively promote cultural development along the Belt and Road and effectively perform the guiding role of mechanism between cultural institutions in countries along the

Belt and Road, the International Alliance of Museums of the Silk Road (IAMS) was formally established, with 110 Chinese member units and 47 foreign member units actively participating so far. The IAMS official website is launched today, which will provide services and convenience for cooperation and communication among museums and cultural heritage protection institutions all over the world.

Today, the grand opening of the IAMS First Conference will continue to promote peace and cooperation, openness and inclusiveness, mutual learning and mutual benefit. It will further enhance the international influence and appeal of building the Belt and Road and will attract more and more countries along the Belt and Road. The conference will provide new opportunities for museums of these countries to share resources, exchange experiences, pool wisdom, and seek common development. It is expected that these countries will continue to further cultural exchanges and cooperation in a close, positive, and friendly direction upholding the principles of extensive consultation, joint contribution, and shared benefits. It is hoped that through our work, exchange will replace estrangement, mutual learning will replace clashes, and coexistence will replace a sense of superiority, and people-to-people exchanges will be strengthened and benefit will be shared by peoples of countries of the Belt and Road Initiative.

Thank you again for your presence. I wish the conference a complete success and I wish you all a pleasant time in Fuzhou!

Opening Speech at the First Conference of the International Alliance of Museums of the Silk Road

Li Chun
Deputy Mayor, Fuzhou Municipal People's Government, Fujian Province, China

Yesterday we saw the opening of the 8th International Exposition of Museums and Relevant Products and Technologies. This morning, we gathered here for the First Conference of the International Alliance of Museums of the Silk Road (IAMS) to build a platform of

communication for museums of the Silk Road, strengthen mutual cooperation, and realize win-win development. Entrusted by Mr. You Mengjun, Mayor of Fuzhou Municipality, on behalf of the People's Government of Fuzhou Municipality, I would like to extend my warm congratulations to the successful convening of the IAMS First Conference and express my heartfelt appreciation to representatives and experts present at this conference!

Rich in history, Fuzhou has been an important starting point for the ancient Maritime Silk Road. Historical literature proves that as early as the Han dynasty, Fuzhou opened traffic routes with the Indochina Peninsula and Japan. Under the rule of Wang Shenzhi and his clan in the Five Dynasties period, Fuzhou actively promoted trade with Korea, Japan, Southeast Asia, and the Arab region. The Ming dynasty maritime explorer Zheng He stationed his fleets at the Taiping Port in Changle and used it as a starting base for his seven voyages to the Indian Ocean. During the Ming to Qing dynasties, tributary trade between China and Ryukyu was conducted mainly through Fuzhou. Fuzhou was deeply engaged in the glorious history of the ancient Maritime Silk Road and has prominent role in the history of Sino-Western trade and cultural exchanges. Abundant historical remains of the Maritime Silk Road can still be found in Fuzhou today. On November 17, 2012, for the first time, six Maritime Silk Road cultural heritage sites in Fuzhou were included in China's World Cultural Heritage Tentative List.

For a long time, with the support of the National Cultural Heritage Administration, the Fuzhou municipal government has been attaching great importance to the protection and utilization of cultural heritage of the Maritime Silk Road and its bid for the World Heritage Status. A working group for the bid has been established, presided over by the Mayor. Fuzhou has joined the alliance of cities for protecting Maritime Silk Road and joint bidding for the World Heritage Status. The Administrative Measures for the Protection of Historic Sites and Cultural Heritage of the Maritime Silk Road in Fuzhou and the Regulations on the Protection of Historic Sites of the Maritime Silk Road in Fuzhou have been published and implemented. In addition, an exhibition center on the Maritime Silk Road is built in Fuzhou and has opened to the public for free. At present, Fuzhou is accelerating the development of "Marine Fuzhou". We have organized large-scale activities such as the Maritime Silk Road Tourism Festival, the

Silk Road International Film Festival, and the 21st Century Maritime Silk Road Expo. We are also continuously carrying out the project "Fuzhou Brands along the Maritime Silk Road", in the interest of promoting city-to-city interconnections, market development, cultural exchanges, etc. and striving to create a strategic fulcrum for the construction of the core area of the Maritime Silk Road. I sincerely hope that the IAMS First Conference will generate insightful new ideas among experts, enlighten the cultural and museum sector, and help promote the cultural and museum development in Fuzhou, especially in the aspects of the protection and utilization of the Maritime Silk Road heritage and its bid for the World Heritage Status!

Finally, I wish the IAMS First Conference a great success.

Conference Papers ▪
大会发言

National Museum of History of Azerbaijan

Naila Valikhanova

Vice President, International Alliance of Museums of the Silk Road

Director, National Museum of History of Azerbaijan

The first steps in the sphere of the state museum formation is directly connected with the functioning of the National Museum of History of Azerbaijan (named as "The State Museum of Azerbaijan SSR" till 1936), the foundation of which was laid down in 1920. On June 15 of that

year the museum has become not only the museum of the country, but scientific-educational center since the very day of its foundation as well.

The Museum engages in collection, storage of the material and spiritual values reflecting the history from the ancient ages till the modern period of Azerbaijan people, and demonstration of them in the expositions, study and publishing. At the present time, there are about 300 thousand exhibits in the museum funds reflecting all periods of the history.

The museum is located in the residential house of Haji Zeynalabdin Taghiyev (1838–1924), the oil proprietor, prominent philanthropist and public figure. The building was projected and constructed in 1895–1901 and was restored from 2005–2007 on initiative and support of Ilham Aliyev, the President of Azerbaijan Republic. The memorial flat of H.Z. Taghiyev functions at the museum till today.

At present, alongside 11 funds, the museum has six academic departments in operation, including archaeology, ethnography and numismatics as well as a restoration laboratory and a library. Besides, many informative publications have taken the museum's collections to a wider mass of readers, such as books, booklets, catalogs, albums and academic publications; in various period, the scholars released works including the richest collection of museum materials. The academic collection published every year includes *Azerbaijan National History Museum* follows in the line of articles, *Azerbaijan National Academy of Science National Museum of History of Azerbaijan* guides, *Gems from the Collection of the National Museum of History of Azerbajan, Garabagh Carpets, Baku, Shirvan and Guba Carpets catalogues*, albums and a number of other publications released as a result of the labor and skills of museum professionals.

The National Museum of History of Azerbaijan has established links with various world museums as well as good cooperation with many research institutes, including those in Russia, Turkey, USA, Germany, China, Norway, Vatican and Czech Republic. The museum has participated in a number of exhibitions, meetings and forums, carried out joint research and personnel exchanges, and held touring exhibitions in Japan, Norway, Czech and other countries.

The National Museum of History of Azerbaijan has a lot of successful experiences in the Silk Road exhibitions, and has carried out many historical studies. In the 19th and 20th centuries, the Silk Road had a huge impact on Azerbaijan. In the collection of the National Museum of History of Azerbaijan, there are many silk textile remains from the ancient Silk Road trade and other Western and Eastern cultural relics related to the Silk Road. In history, goods from China and India came to Azerbaijan through the Silk Road. At that time, trade was very important and had a significant impact on Azerbaijan. From the 13th to 15th centuries, cultural and economic exchanges between China and Azerbaijan continued to grow, with many envoys travelling between the two countries. In the collection of the National Museum of History of Azerbaijan, there are many national treasures obtained through archaeological excavations, which include imported ceramics, furniture, tea wares, etc. from China. The bowls, silk, jewels and weapons imported from China and East Asian countries were very popular in Azerbaijan at that time and had become an indispensable part of people's daily life. In the capital of Azerbaijan, the imported Chinese porcelain, with their distinctive Chinese characteristics, have always been popular and expensive, because in the Middle Ages, the technique of porcelain production was very rare.

In the 18th and 19th centuries, our histories were closely connected with each other, and people's lives were greatly enriched through commercial trade and cultural exchanges. In conclusion, the Silk Road has had a profound impact on Azerbaijan. In the future, the National Museum of History of Azerbaijan would continue to explore historical relics, finding examples of the integration of different civilizations.

Dr. Naila Valikhanova

Vice President, International Alliance of Museums of the Silk Road

Director, National Museum of History of Azerbaijan

Naila Valikhanova is doctor of history, academician from 2007, member of ICOM. Her main scientific investigation revealed problems of source study of Azerbaijan History of the Middle Ages, situation of region within Arab Caliphate, social-economic relation, political-cultural history and historical geography. She had achieved success in historiography of Azerbaijan after having demolished Armenian and Georgian arguments dominating in science until recently. She published more than 248 scientific articles and books, 19 of which were printed abroad. She took part in national and international conferences and has got several awards and prizes.

National Museum of the Republic of Kazakhstan

Satubaldin Abay Karemtaevich

Deputy Director, National Museum of the Republic of Kazakhstan

The National Museum of the Republic of Kazakhstan is interested in establishing close cooperation with the leading foreign museums and the host museum to foster cooperation with museums along the Silk Road.

The National Museum of Kazakhstan was opened on July 2, 2014 as part of the implementation of the State Program "Cultural Heritage". It is the youngest and largest museum in the country. The total area of the museum is 74,000 square meters, with an exposition area of 14,000 square meters. The expositions of the National Museum tell about the history of Kazakhstan since ancient times to modern times. The museum has 10 stationary halls and 6 halls for temporary exhibitions. The Archaeology Hall displays the rich history and culture of Kazakhstan; the Independent Kazakhstan Hall shows the process of Kazakhstan's journey towards independence and development; the Astana Hall displays the culture of the country during the Astana period through important artifacts and documents; the Modern Art Halls illustrates the cultural evolution of Kazakhstan in the process of modernization with exhibitions of different schools of contemporary art, visual art and sculptures.

The Museum has 531 employees, spreading in 14 structural divisions, including research institutes, restoration workshops and laboratories, scientific library. There are over 200,000 museum objects, among which are seven "Golden Warriors" from the Scythian-Saka period.

The National Museum has become one of the most visited cultural locations of the capital. In four years functioning, over 3 million people have visited the museum. Every year, the museum holds a large number of international and public cultural events, including exhibitions, conferences, forums, lectures, museum lessons, festivals and round tables.

As we all know that in the ancient times, the Great Silk Road passed through the territory of modern Kazakhstan. The Great Silk Road was the bridge between the East and the West, along which a large number of the medieval cities functioned. The medieval cities such as Taraz, Turkestan and others are known on the territory of Kazakhstan. Kazakhstan archaeologists excavated on the medieval cities along the route of the Silk Road and discovered archaeological finds that show the cultural agreements and exchanges among countries. A large number of artifacts are stored in our museum.

Kazakhstan included 8 archaeological monuments in the UNESCO World Heritage List within the framework of the Transnational Serial Nomination "Silk Roads: the Routes Network of Chang'an-Tianshan Corridor", which was proposed by Kazakhstan together with China and Kyrgyzstan. As part of this project, there was the joint exhibition *Miles upon Miles: World Heritage along the Silk Road* at the Hong Kong Museum of History in 2017. The exhibition is dedicated to the archaeological monuments located on the Silk Road. Objects from the museums of Kazakhstan, China and Kyrgyzstan have been presented at this exhibition.

In concluding my statement, I would like to comment on the cooperation with the International Alliance of Museums of the Silk Road and development of a joint work plan. Let me repeat again that National Museum of the Republic of Kazakhstan is interested in cooperation and is ready to join the International Alliance of Museums of the Silk Road. With regard to our proposals to the plan of work of the International Alliance of Museums of the Silk Road, I would like to mention traditional forms of inter-museum cooperation, including organizing and conducting seminars and training for young museum specialists, carrying out scientific researches, organizing joint exhibitions and conferences, as well as other events.

Mr. Satubaldin Abay Karemtaevich

Deputy Director, National Museum of the Republic of Kazakhstan

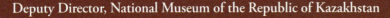

Education Background:

June 2011　Completed internship at Sanford School of Public Policy, Duke University, USA.

2010-2012　Graduated with honors from the Academy of Public Administration under the President of the Republic of Kazakhstan, Master of Public and Local Administration.

September-October 2009　Completed a short-term training programme on the subject State Policy in the Sphere of Culture at the St. Petersburg State University of Culture and Art, Russia.

2006-2008　Graduated with honors from the L.N. Gumilyov Eurasian National University, Master of Archeology and Ethnology.

2003-2004　Passed the military department of the L.N. Gumilyov Eurasian National University with reserve lieutenant rank.

2000-2004　Graduated with honors from the L.N. Gumilyov Eurasian National University, major "Archeology and Ethnology".

Professional Experience:

2015 to present　Deputy Director of the National Museum of the Republic of Kazakhstan.

2014-2015　Chief Expert of the Department of Culture and Arts of the Ministry of Culture and Sports of the Republic of Kazakhstan.

2008-2014　Chief Expert of the Committee on Culture of the Ministry of Culture of the Republic of Kazakhstan.

2007-2008　Chief Specialist of Historical and Cultural Heritage Department at the Ministry of Culture and Information of the Republic of Kazakhstan.

2005-2007　Senior Researcher at the Museum of the First President of the Republic of Kazakhstan.

2004-2005　Chief Curator, Senior Researcher at the Presidential Center of Culture.

National Museum of Cambodia

Kong Vireak

Director, National Museum of Cambodia

Located in Phnom Penh, the capital of Cambodia, the National Museum of Cambodia is the first museum in Cambodian history. The museum was not conceived simply as a place to conserve and display collections. From the beginning it was integrally linked to the contiguous School of Cambodian Arts (École des arts cambodgiens), whose mission was to train artisans in diverse skills. Such was the vision of its founder, George Groslier, who intended that objects from antiquity would provide a source of inspiration for a modern art that he considered somewhat sluggish after a long sleep, yet potentially powerful. That is why one finds 19th and 20th century objects of everyday life, not without artistic value, in the museum. Apprentices in jewelry, metal-casting, drawing, sculpting, weaving worked then in a most propitious atmosphere. It must also be said that antiquities had already begun to disappear from sites on their way to various foreign collections, legal controls for their protection doubtless still being uncertain. Ever since, the organization of a museum has clearly been ever more indispensable.

In 1917, the first stone of the Cambodian museum was solemnly laid, thus launching the project. Construction was completed in 1920, followed by the inauguration of the museum, then called "The Albert Sarraut Museum". Regardless of its first collections, the building itself was already perceived as a work of great distinction. The opinion was unanimous.

In 1951, the French Protectorate entrusted the responsibility for the management of the heritage to the Khmer authorities, and the museum was renamed "The National Museum of Cambodia". However, the museum was directed by a succession of French directors until 1966, when the first Cambodian was put in charge.

Since its establishment, the National Museum of Cambodia has been dedicated to collecting archaeological and ethnographic objects, including stone, wood, metal, ceramics, etc. The museum's collection is continuously enriched. A number of guides, as well as various catalogues and publications relevant to the collections, are already known to the public.

The National Museum of Cambodia houses one of the world's greatest collections of Khmer cultural heritage including sculpture, ceramics and ethnographic objects from the prehistoric, pre-Angkor, Angkor and Post-Angkor periods. The collection mainly consists of stone, wood and metal sculptures related to Hinduism and Buddhism, but the museum also holds collections of ceramics, ethnographic objects, textiles, paintings and ceremonial objects.

The collection of the Cambodian Museum is rich and spans different historical periods,

including the Pre-Angkorian period from 5th-6th to the end of 8th century, the Angkor period from 9th to the late 14th century, the Post-Angkor period from 15th to middle 19th century, and the Modern period after 19th century which is influenced by the western art style. In the Bronze Galleries, there are 11th century 6-meter-high statues, as well as kneeling female figure and adorned Buddha, etc. The Sculpture Gallery displays religious statues of Hinduism, Buddhism and Christianity in the early 6th century. There are also the late 10th century sculpture of Shiva, the goddess of snow mountain, and the 13th-14th century sculpture of Yama. The Wooden and Ethnographic Gallery mainly displays collections from 18th to late 19th century, including woodcarving crafts and sculptures, etc. Paintings of late 19th century are exhibited in the Painting Gallery, most of which are influenced by French colonialism, but different from those in the West painted with unique traditional techniques.

Regarding to the relationship between the National Museum of Cambodia and the International Alliance of Museums of the Silk Road, the following questions may be raised: whether Cambodian art and handicrafts reflect the theme of the Silk Road. Although Chinese historical documentations have constantly attested the envoys and diplomatic situations of the two countries, the relations and connections between China and Cambodia are still abstract. Cambodian civilization is characterized by strong influences of two major civilizations, India and China, among which Indian influences is quite obvious from art to architecture, from religion to kingship, from language to philosophy, etc. However, China's influence on Cambodia is intangible. One is hard to see Chinese images or elements in Khmer culture and civilization except a huge quantity of imported Chinese ceramics; while other aspects can be seen through trading system, calculation, measurement etc. One may amazingly impress. The National Museum of Cambodia has few collections to show the connections with the Silk Road. But there is a 13th century relief in Bayon, depicting the scene of a Chinese boat and its owner. It can be seen that there were Chinese people on the boat, whose headdress and clothes are different from those of the local people, might be Chinese businessmen who come to Cambodia for trade.

Above is the basic information of the National Museum of Cambodia. There are many cultural relics and remains of the Tang and Ming dynasties in Cambodia, as well as some Fujian collections of art. It hopes that National Museum of Cambodia will hold more exchanging exhibitions with China in the future.

Mr. Kong Vireak

Director, National Museum of Cambodia

Kong Vireak is the Director of the Department of Museums, Ministry of Culture and Fine Arts and Director of the National Museum of Cambodia. He graduated with Bachelor degree in archaeology from Department of Archaeology, Royal University of Fine-Arts in Phnom Penh. He received a MA degree in 1998 in cultural anthropology from École des Hautes-Études des Sciences Sociales (EHESS) in Paris. From 1998 to 2005, he worked in Angkor with Japanese Government Team for Safeguarding Angkor. From 2005 to 2012, he served as Director of Education Service of the Royal University of Fine Arts, and later as Vice-Rector. In November 2012, he was appointed as Director of the Department of Museums of the Ministry of Culture and Fine Arts.

Lao National Museum

Phetmalayvanh Keobounma

Director, Lao National Museum

The Lao National Museum in Vientiane is housed in one of the oldest remaining colonial buildings in Laos. Built in 1925, the building continued to be used by the royal government for meetings and ceremonies until 1975, when the country became independent. The exhibition hall was established in 1980 and became the Lao Revolutionary Museum in 1985. In 2000, the museum was converted to the current Lao National Museum. On December 1, 2017, the museum held an opening ceremony for its new building on the occasion of the country's 42nd National Day.

The museum currently stores more than 28,000 registered artefacts and some 130,000 unregistered artefacts, including paintings, stones, copperwares, woodenwares, ironwares, porcelains, etc. The museum also houses exhibits such as goblets and jade wares that reflect the history of the Silk Road.

The Lao National Museum retells Lao history from pre-historic period to today, paying particular focus to the country's culture history and natural environment. The Museum serves as a window to the country and for the Lao nation it provides all aspects in which we are able to protect and develop Laos' collective memory. Since 2000, every year thousands of visitors at home and abroad, scholars and groups of school children visited the museum.

Due to limited storage place, the government had planned to build a new museum building. The newly constructed building is located near the residence of Laos' former president, Lao Central Library, National University of Laos. There are three floors in the new museum building, featuring five exhibition themes including Pre-History, Lan Xang Kingdom, Modern History, Development and Protection, and Lao Ethnic Groups. The Museum is making new exhibition plans as it moves to the new building, and will carefully choose exhibits according to themes and exhibition requirements. Archaeologists and historians from Japan were invited to host lectures and seminars and to participate in study tours of historic remains during the preparation work.

In the future, the Lao National Museum hopes to further develop the new museum building to store and preserve national collections, train professional personnel, upgrade existing exhibitions and host new exhibitions to improve visitor experience. In addition, the museum plans to develop new storage facilities and upgrade conservation labs to preserve its collections. The museum has also established foreign scholarships and other cooperation projects to support research and development. The Lao National Museum hopes to learn from all friendly partners, especially those with rich experience, to improve its work in the future. The museum also looks forwards to exchange work experience with members of the International Alliance of Museums of the Silk Road.

Mrs. Phetmalayvanh Keobounma

Director, Lao National Museum

Educational Background:

1982-1987   Master (M.A) of Art, Oriol University, Russia

Professional Experience:

1990 to present Director of the Lao National Museum

1987-1990   Division of Foreign Affairs, Ministry of Information, Culture and
Tourism, Lao PDR

Project:

Member of the Lao's Exhibition Experts for the MuSEA Program, sponsored by SIDA, a program of Museum Cooperation in Southeast Asia (Laos, Vietnam, Cambodia and Sweden).

National Museum of Myanmar (Yangon)

Daw Nang Lao Ngin

Vice President, International Alliance of Museums of the Silk Road

Director, National Museum of Myanmar (Yangon)

There are over 30 museums in Myanmar, including national museums, archaeological museums, memorial museums, religious museums, regional museums, theme museums and private museums, which are all managed by the Ministry of Religious Affairs and Culture.

Founded in 1871, the Phayre Museum is Myanmar's first museum, and the Bagan Site Museum was established in 1902, the Mrauk U Site Museum was founded in 1905.

The National Museum of Myanmar (Yangon) (NMMY), was established in June 1952 following Myanmar gained its independence in 1948. It was relocated twice in 1968 and 1993 and reopened to the public at 66/74, Pyay Road, Dagon Township, Yangon on 18 September 1996. The present NMMY is a five-story building, 80 feet high, 76,000 square feet of floor space, and 194,800 square feet exhibition space. The museum has 13 exhibition halls. The main exhibition hall is the Lion Throne Room, a symbol of power. In 1957, the Lion Throne Room was transferred from the Royal Family to the NMMY. In the Throne Room, miniature models of the eight kinds of thrones of ancient Myanmar kings and the original Royal Lion Throne of the last monarch are displayed.

Myanmar's cultural policy is to preserve a diverse cultural heritage, which includes tangible and intangible cultural heritage. As a national museum, the NMMY's mission is to explore and collect Myanmar cultural heritage objects to be displayed and preserved. Its vision is to be a centre for people to learn Myanmar culture and its civilization process so as to shape a better future by safeguarding the cultural heritage of Myanmar. The National Museum (Yangon) is now carrying out five functions – collection, preservation and conservation of museum properties, research and publication, displaying (permanent and temporary), public education.

The NMMY currently has more than 700,000 objects in the collection. In accordance with Myanmar's state regulations, the National Museum is responsible for collecting various relics, together with paintings and handicrafts. There are five sources of Museum's collection: purchase, donation, handover, exchange and auction. Institutional and private donations are the main sources.

In the spirit of carrying out conservation and protecting the national treasures, the NMMY focuses not only on museum objects, zone protection, inventory survey, artifacts collection, registration of tangible cultural heritage but also has connection with international organizations like UNESCO and ASEAN, organizing various activities.

The NMMY transmits information to schools and the general public through research and publication, which is very important for museums. The outcome of the researches is conducted on the subjects and published in the form of catalogues, brochures and books. Publications in the form of reports, guide books, pamphlets, etc. are used to familiarize the people with museum and its activities. Special publications on the occasion of special exhibitions and anniversaries are used to popularize the museum with the community. In addition, in order to spread Myanmar's culture, the NMMY conducted a series of training courses on relics and culture. Since 2002, universities in Myanmar began to teach museum courses.

As one of the most significant functions of the museum, exhibitions are very important to international cultural communications. According to the cultural exchange program, many exhibitions have been held in coordination with other foreign countries. It is worth mentioning that the NMMY once held *Exhibition to Commemorate the 55th Anniversary of Myanmar-China Diplomatic Relations* in June 2005. In addition, many local exhibitions are held. The Museum had taken responsibility for holding the United Nation Day exhibition as State Exhibition.

In order to build its organizational structure and improve the current situation of museums in Myanmar, the NMMY, which is managed by the Ministry of Religious Affairs and Culture, has cooperated extensively with other ministries and institutions and actively sought advanced technical support from other countries. Myanmar and China have established close ties for a long time. Culture serves as a bridge to promote friendly exchanges between the two countries, and the cooperation contributes to world cultural exchanges. In the future, museums of the two countries can conduct in-depth cooperation through signing of Memorandum of Understanding, exchange of knowledge and arts, exchange of exhibitions, training of personnel, and organizing children's education projects. It is hoped that the museums of the two countries will strengthen cooperation and become models for ASEAN countries.

Daw Nang Lao Ngin

Vice President, International Alliance of Museums of the Silk Road

Director, National Museum of Myanmar (Yangon)

Educational Background:

December, 2017　Graduated from the National University of Arts and Culture, Yangon, Myanmar, M.A. in Museology

December, 2009　Graduated from the National University of Arts and Culture, Yangon, Myanmar, Diploma in Museology

Professional Experience:

2015 to present　Director, National Museum of Myanmar (Yangon): Management of Museum in all function

1992-2015　Subsequently Curator Great (2), Staff Officer, Assistant Director, Deputy Director, Director, Shan State Cultural Museum (Taunggyi): Management of Museum Work such as Collection, Research for Ethnic Group in Shan State, Display, Education

Academic Achievements:

Basic Diplomatic Skills Training Course, Ministry of Foreign Affair in Yangon (03.10.2017-29.12.2017)

Ratifying the 2005 Convention UNESCO Workshop in Nay Pyi Taw (24-26.11.2017)

Myanmar National ICH List to UNESCO Nomination List Training Course in Taunggyi (14-18.10.2015)

Public Policy and Administrative Reform at Singapore Training School (04-08.05.2015)

Community Base Inventory Workshop with UNESCO in Nyaungshwe, Shan State (27.10.2014-03.11.2014)

Israel Antiquities Authority

Orit Shamir

Head, Department of Museums and Exhibits, Israel Antiquities Authority

Israel is a very young country, there are around 350 archaeological museums, exhibitions and outdoor exhibitions around the country, some of which are decades old. Though many archaeological sites have been discovered along with the development of the country, museums

in Israel have very limited collections. For exhibitions, museums need to borrow relics from the government, some may also come from other museums, public institutions, hospitals or hotels.

This conference is important for Israel's museums, which are looking for new approaches to present and introduce cultural heritages to the public, especially how to educate the young generation.

Israel is a small country, so museums have very close connections to government institutions. The Israel Antiquities Authority also maintains friendly relations with other countries, lending many cultural relics to overseas museums and keeping good cooperation with Chinese museums.

I appreciate this opportunity to get to know many outstanding colleagues and friends from China and the International Alliance of Museums of the Silk Road.

Dr. Orit Shamir

Head, Department of Museums and Exhibits, Israel Antiquities Authority

Orit Shamir, Dr. phil. (Jerusalem 2007) is Head of the Department of Museums and Exhibits and Curator of Organic Materials at the Israel Antiquities Authority. Her area of specialization is ancient textiles, loomweights and spindle-whorls from Neolithic to the Medieval period in Israel. She has been invited to give lectures and papers at many academic and public events, they are listed at: antiquities.academia.edu/OritShamir.

National Historical Museum of the Republic of Belarus

Luda Tolkacheva

Head of the Department of Archeology, Numismatics and Weapon

National Historical Museum of the Republic of Belarus

The National Historical Museum of the Republic of Belarus is the largest museum in the country, with a collection of more than 460,000 items, distributed over 58 collections. The museum's history can be traced back to 1919. With its name changed several times throughout

the history, the museum was renamed as "National Museum of History and Culture of Belarus" in 1992, and was changed to "National Historical Museum of the Republic of Belarus" in 2009 which is still in use today. During the Second World War, the collection of the National Historical Museum of the Republic of Belarus suffered damage. After the War, the collection was transferred to Germany, and only a small part of about 2% of the collection was able to returned to Belarus, thus, the collection number was enormously deceased.

The museum includes five branches: Memorial House of the First Congress of Russian Social Democratic Labour Party, the Museum of Belarusian Cinema History, the Museum of the Theatre and Musical Culture History of the Republic of Belarus, the Museum of Contemporary Belarusian Statehood, the Museum of Nature and Ecology. All these became the branches of the National Historical Museum of the Republic of Belarus in 2014. Each of the branches has a permanent exhibition, own exhibition halls and conducts cultural and educational programs in accordance with its own specifics.

The main activities of the museum are: acquisition of museum funds, accounting, storage and restoration of museum items, scientific and auxiliary materials; creation and opening of temporary expositions, modernization of permanent expositions of branches; study, use and popularization of museum items, scientific and auxiliary materials; excursion services for museum visitors, cultural and educational work and cultural and educational activities; conducting and participating in scientific and practical seminars and conferences, other events in the field of museum business; organization of international cultural projects; implementation of methodological work, provision of consulting assistance to regional museums of local history and natural history.

There is a certain connection between the collection of the National Historical Museum of the Republic of Belarus and the Silk Road. Part of the collection is obtained from archaeological excavations in countries along the Silk Road, mainly including jewelry, household wares, ceramics, coins and weapons, etc. Most of these collections have never been exhibited abroad. It is hoped that through the platform of the International Alliance of Museums of the Silk Road, the National Historical Museum of the Republic of Belarus would have more opportunities to hold cultural exchange exhibitions in the future and achieve further developments and exchanges with China and other Silk Road countries, exhibiting museum collections to Chinese general public, as well as presenting rich cultural heritage of Belarus to audience worldwide.

Dr. Luda Tolkacheva

Head of the Department of Archaeology, Numismatics and Weapon

National Historical Museum of the Republic of Belarus

Educational Background:

Since 2016	PhD in Art Criticism, Belarusian State Academy of Arts
2009-2012	Postgraduate studies, Belarusian State Academy of Arts
2008-2009	Master of Arts (focused on Belarusian art metal of religious use), Belarusian State Academy of Arts
2002-2007	Bachelor in Fine Arts (focused on decorative and applied arts, church vessels), Historical faculty of Belarusian State University

Professional Experience:

2018 to present	Board Member, National Historical Museum of the Republic of Belarus
2016 to present	Head of the Department of Archeology, Numismatics and Weapon
2010 to present	National Historical Museum of the Republic of Belarus

Scientific Interests:

Belarusian art metal, Belarusian numismatics, international financial relations of Belarusian territories in 16th – 17th centuries.

Participation in Conferences and Publications:

Took part at about 20 national and international conferences, including: The Third

Scientific Readings in Memory of Professor Valentine Ryabtsevich, Belarus, Minsk, 2018; VIII International Numismatic Conference, Belarus, Minsk-Raubichi, 2017; XIX All-Russian Numismatic Conference, Russia, Veliki Novgorod, 2017.

Author of 17 publications in peer reviewed journals and scientific digests of articles:

Sukhareuski Hoard of coins of Polish-Lithuanian Commonwealth and Prussia of the 2nd half of 17th – 1st half of 18th cent (in Russian) in Bank Bulletin Magazine, #2 2018.

Brodok Hoard of coins of the 1st half of the 16th century of Polish-Lithuanian Commonwealth and Western Europe from National Historical Museum of the Republic of Belarus (in Russian) in Digest of Articles of the Third Scientific Readings in Memory of Professor Valentine Ryabtsevich, Minsk, 2018.

Numismatic Exhibition "From Roman Denarius to Belarussian Rouble" in the National Historical Museum of the Republic of Belarus (in Russian) in Digest of Articles of The XIX All-Russian Numismatic Conference, Moscow, 2017.

Institute of Nasledie (Stravropol) Ltd.

Zvezdana Dode

Senior Researcher, Institute of Nasledie (Stravropol) Ltd.

Founded in 1995, the Institute of Nasledie (Stravropol) Ltd. is a professional institute. Its activities encompass archaeological research of historical and cultural monuments, identification of historical and cultural monuments in the areas zoned out for development and construction, conservation of antiquities and archaeological textiles, and development and deployment of geo-information technologies for archaeological research.

The Silk Road spanned from China, extended through Russia and reached as far as Europe, and many cultural relics from China were found along the way in Russia, including Chinese silk. Many cultural institutions in Russia and China have jointly carried out a number of research projects on the themes of the Silk Road, the collections along the Silk Road, and the Silk Road archaeology. The Institute of Nasledie (Stravropol) Ltd., for instance, has collaborated with the China National Silk Museum to work on the examination and conservation of Mongolian textiles. Some existing projects also achieved new progress. A number of museums and institutions in Russia have joined in associations for the Silk Road study. The Institute of Nasledie (Stravropol) Ltd. has actively participated in symposiums and seminars hosted by the International Association for the Study of Silk Roads Textiles (IASSRT). In November 2018, the 3rd IASSRT Symposium was successfully hosted in Buyeo, Korea. The 4th IASSRT Symposium will be hosted in September 2019 in Russia, jointly organized by the Institute of Nasledie (Stravropol) Ltd. and the State Hermitage Museum in St. Petersburg.

We sincerely welcome and invite all representatives to give more attention and support to the research of and cooperation with the Institute of Nasledie (Stavropol) Ltd. in Russia.

Dr. Zvezdana Dode

Senior Researcher, Institute of Nasledie (Stravropol) Ltd.

Area of Expertise:

Medieval costume and textiles of the North Caucasus and Central Asia

Educational Background:

Ph. D, The Oriental Institute, Russian Academy of Science, Moscow

M.A. in Archaeology, Stavropol State University, Stavropol

B.A. in History, Education, Stavropol State University, Stavropol

Professional Experience:

2018 to present	Senior Researcher, Institute of Nasledie (Stravropol) Ltd.
	Senior Researcher, Research Institute of Archaeology and Ancient History of the North Caucasus (Stavropol, Russia)
2011-2018	Senior Researcher, Southern Scientific Center of Russian Academy of Sciences (SSC RAS)
1997-2010	Professor of Archaeology and Art History, Stavropol State University
1994-1997	Curator of the Department of Archaeology, Stavropol State Museum
1987-1997	Head of the Department of Archaeology, Stavropol State Museum
1980-1982	Archivist, Stavropol State Archives

Transformation: National Museum in Belgrade, Republic of Serbia

Bojana Borić-Brešković

Vice President, International Alliance of Museums of the Silk Road

Director, National Museum in Belgrade, Republic of Serbia

The National Museum in Belgrade is the largest and the oldest museum in Serbia. It is founded in 1844 as Serbian Museum (Muzeum serbski). After the Second World War, in 1950, the Museum was granted the former State Mortgage Bank's building, where it remained to

this very day, and after a brief repair, opened for general public in 1952. From 2015 to 2018, the museum once again completely renovated the building, ushering in a new chapter of development.

The National Museum in Belgrade is a complex museum devoted to the protection, interpretation and promotion of the layered, multicultural heritage of the central Balkans and Europe - a culture from prehistory to the present - through archaeological, numismatic and artistic materials. The museum collects, preserves, protects against the principles of preventive protection, improve knowledge. It interprets historical and contemporary cultures, serving as a source of knowledge and an active center of learning in the community and environment.

The National Museum was and should be the most important museological center in the Balkans, role model for other museums in the country and the region. And it should be a national cultural center of regional and worldwide importance, an inevitable and favorite destination for Belgrade citizens and tourists from the country and the world, recognizable in public.

The National Museum inspires and encourages curiosity. The permanent display represents common energy, a collective creative activity in which different specialists have their place. At the same time, the museum is displayed as a public forum where all museum activities can be seen, from research and conservation to interpretation and education. In the new permanent exhibition, the most significant and most intriguing segments of the archaeological, numismatic and art collections are exhibited.

The missions of the new permanent exhibition are to present and in its own way interprets and preserves longlasting values confirmed by history as well as research of the museum audience and future visitors, to use chronological flow to present the continuity and discontinuity of cultural and historical development in the region, to present live cultural contacts and their mutual interweaving and permeation, and to present the most significant and most intriguing segments of the 30 archaeological, numismatic and art collections. The new permanent exhibition of the Museum showcases the works in the context - chronological, geographical, artistic, cultural, social and scientific, informs, sensitizes, and develops feelings for ethical and aesthetic values, contributes to understanding identity, educates the spirit, develops awareness of the past.

The criterion for the success of a museum exhibition, a museum setting should be whether it has managed to achieve an emotional experience, including new attitudes and interests, and not whether visitors came out of the museum by learning specific facts or understanding the principles of a scientific discipline. Although museum exhibitions should be educational and entertaining (for enjoyment) at the same time, and their purpose is to transform some aspects of the visitor's interests, attitudes, or values emotionally, thanks to his discovery of a new level of significance in exposed objects which rooted in the visitor's trust in the authenticity of objects.

Among the highlights of collection covering span of more than 500,000 years, are statues of god and goddesses from Lepenski Vir (7th millennium B.C.), the Vinca statues (6-5th millennium B.C.), the Dupljaja Chariot (16-13th century B.C.), golden masks and bonze crate from Trebeniste (6th century B.C.), the Belgrade Cameo (4th century), bronze head of Constantine the Great (4th century), Miroslav's Gospel (12th century), Radoslav's coins (13th century), medieval orthodox frescoes and icons, enamel plaques from Hilandar (15th century), numerous Serbian and Yugoslav works of art, from artist such as Uroš Predić, Pavle Jovanović (19th century), Nadežda Petrović, Sava Šumanović or Ivan Mestrović (20th century), as well as striking masterpieces of Carpaccio, Rubens, Degas, Renoir, Matisse, Picasso, Mondrian.

The most significant evidence for understanding of archaeology and history of art, representing development and changes of civilization in the territory of today's Serbia and its immediate surroundings, from prehistoric times to late medieval period, as well as crucial artistic tendencies and styles, supreme artistic merits in national and European art, from medieval period to contemporary works, will be given in innovative ways of display, creating new ways of thinking about archaeology and art, new ways of thinking about identity of Serbia, new ways of seeing and understanding the world we live in.

Developing on the Balkan Peninsula, Serbia has been in the past, as it is today, the place of merging and interweaving of people and cultures. It is a place of cultural interaction between the regions for many centuries. For that reason, through history it was perceived as railroad,

highway or the bridge between East and West, Asia and Europe.

Today, people, information, goods, etc. are moving faster than ever before. The National Museum in Belgrade hopes to continue its tradition by interpreting the history of the past centuries in an understandable and readable way. We hope that in the 21st century we will continue to be a channel, a road, a bridge and to successfully transfer knowledge and merge cultures as what we have been doing since the beginning.

Ms. Bojana Borić-Brešković

Vice President, International Alliance of Museums of the Silk Road

Director, National Museum in Belgrade, Republic of Serbia

Graduated in the Classics, parallel with studies in archaeology, from the Faculty of Philosophy at Belgrade University. She went on to earn a master's degree at the faculty's Department of History. During her career at the Museum she has been a curator in the post of museum advisor, and Director of the National Museum in Belgrade (from 2012 onwards). She was appointed Secretary of Culture of the City of Belgrade (1994-1996), and Director of the National Museum in Belgrade (1996-2001). Her particular field of study is the history of the cultures and the economic history of the Central Balkans in the period of Antiquity. On several occasions, her research has taken her abroad to other European museums and research institutions. She has organized or participated in organizing a large number of exhibitions and other events. She has also collaborated with or headed teams in several scientific and research projects.

Where the Chinese Dream Begins: National Museum of China

Huang Zhenchun

Secretary General, International Alliance of Museums of the Silk Road

Deputy Director, National Museum of China

The National Museum of China (NMC) is China's supreme establishment that collects, researches, displays and interprets China's fine traditional culture, revolutionary culture and advanced socialist culture. It preserves the collective memory of the nation and interprets

its outstanding cultural identity. The museum houses more than 1.4 million objects as the embodiment and witness of Chinese people's memory of history and reality, and their vision for the future. As a cultural lounge for China, the NMC receives as many as nearly 8 million visitors per year, it plays an important role in spreading and promoting Chinese culture, and boosting communication and exchanges among Chinese and foreign civilizations.

Since the museum's reopening after renovation in 2011, President Xi Jinping has made five visits to the NMC and delivered important speeches. The NMC is also where President Xi Jinping first called for realizing the Chinese Dream.

In 2018, the NMC completed *The Road of Rejuvenation: New Era* and held two major thematic exhibitions: *The Power of Truth – An Exhibition Marking the Bicentenary of the Birth of Karl Marx,* and *Great Changes: A Major Exhibition Commemorating the 40th Anniversary of China's Reform and Opening-up*. For international exchanges, several exhibitions have been launched, such as *To Commemorate the 100th Anniversary of the October Revolution: Objects of the October Revolution from the State Historical Museum of Russia, The Power of Innovation: Patent Models from the United States of America, Embracing the Orient and the Occident: When the Silk Road Meets the Renaissance*, and the *Old Masters: Australia's Great Bark Artists*. In early 2018, we participated in a cooperative exhibition at the National Museum of Korea, and in December, the NMC is going to hold an exhibition of *Life in the Midst of Beauty: The World of a Chinese Scholar* at the National Museum in Belgrade, Serbia.

About the future development of the NMC, we made plans from different aspects as follows:

Firstly, to explore the development of museum's main and branch construction. The main and branch development of museum is becoming a trend, and it is also an important opportunity for promoting high-quality development of museums. Through the combination of the main museum and its branches, exhibitions and cultural relics could be revitalized, thus the innovation of the museum's management system and operation mechanism will be realized, which is conducive to promoting the coordinated development of culture, cultural relics and tourism. At present, the NMC has decided to set branches in Xiong'an New Area and

Shenzhen, and various work is progressing steadily.

Secondly, to promote the development of Smart NMC. The NMC has proposed the goal of building a smart museum, which will bring cultural relics to life through modern technology such as big data, cloud computing, Internet of Things, virtual reality and artificial intelligence. At the same time, the informatization and intellectualization of museum management and service will also be promoted and achieve a leapfrog.

Thirdly, to strengthen means of innovative dissemination. In the Internet era, the NMC will continue to strengthen the innovation of dissemination means and forms, to promote the development of multimedia content, and to increase guidance, influence and credibility in public opinion. Furthermore, the museum aims to improve the ability of telling characteristic stories in appropriate ways and methods, as well as to strengthen the museum's public education function, thus to expand and enhance exhibitions' social benefits.

Fourthly, to implement the curator-centered exhibition system. The curator-centered exhibition system is more than a policy on talent resources, but also a profound institutional reform in museum field. The NMC will, through the implementation of this system, further highlight its exhibition function, which is the main business and responsibility of the museum.

Fifthly, to promote inter-museum cooperation. The NMC shall strengthen communication and establish strategic partnerships with local museums, and promote the normalization and institutionalization of loan exhibitions and important tour exhibitions in accordance with the principle of "aspiring not to how many is collected but how many is exhibited, embracing openness and cooperation for mutual benefits"; continue to increase cooperation with foreign cultural institutions, especially various national museums, to carry out international tour exhibitions and hold international forums, in order to promote exchanges and mutual learning.

A museum is an important hall for the protection and inheritance of human civilization and also a bridge connecting the past, the present and the future. It has a special role in promoting exchanges and mutual learning among world civilizations, and the IAMS aims at enhancing this feature.

Since the Secretariat of IAMS was reassigned to the NMC in June 2018, with the joint efforts of all members, we have further clarified the responsibilities, mechanism and responsibilities of the IAMS Secretariat; drafted the Statutes of the International Alliance of Museums of the Silk Road, established the IAMS website. All these work laid a solid foundation for the successful convening of today's conference.

In 2019, the IAMS will focus on the following aspects of work:

Firstly, to strengthen platform construction. To continuously improve the liaison mechanism, give full play to the coordination role of the Secretariat, and ensure the continuation and deepening of cooperation projects.

Secondly, to increase exhibition cooperation. Exhibitions and forums will be launched and conducted in succession, such as the joint exhibition of the Belt and Road national museums on the theme of exchanges and mutual learning among civilizations, the Global Museum Directors Forum, the exhibition of *Life along the Silk Road,* and the Curator's Forum: Collaboration on the Silk Road Exhibitions.

Thirdly, to promote exchanges and training events. According to the practical needs, we shall organize professionals' exchange visits among members, and conduct in-depth thematic exchanges and training events, thereby to inspire each other, and share academic resources and achievements.

Fourthly, to implement joint publishing. To make maximum use of the IAMS members' advantages in collections, resources and talents to conduct joint research and joint publications.

From now on, let us work together as good partners and friends. As a Chinese saying goes, "separated as we are thousands of miles apart, we come together as if by predestination." Today, we all gather here with colleagues from cultural institutions home and abroad, it is a kind of indissoluble bond that crosses geographical boundaries. We shall value this opportunity to deepen our friendship, and further contribute to the development of human civilization and the welfare of mankind.

Proceedings of the First Conference of
the International Alliance of Museums of the Silk Road

Mr. Huang Zhenchun

Secretary General, International Alliance of Museums of the Silk Road

Deputy Director, National Museum of China

Educational Background:

July, 1983   Graduated from Nankai University, majoring in political economy

Professional Experience:

February, 2009-February, 2019   Deputy Director, National Museum of China

July, 2005-February, 2009   Director of Department of General Affairs, Ministry of Culture

July, 1996-July, 2005   Deputy Director of Department of General Affairs, Ministry of Culture

December, 1992-July, 1996   Secretary of General Office, Propaganda Department, CPC Central Committee; Secretary of Department of General Affairs, Ministry of Culture

July, 1983-December, 1992   Cadre of State Education Commission, renamed later as the "Ministry of Education"; Secretary of General Office, State Council; Secretary of General Office, Propaganda Department, CPC Central Committee

International Collaboration along the Silk Road: China National Silk Museum

Zhao Feng

Vice President, International Alliance of Museums of the Silk Road

Director, China National Silk Museum

Established in 1992, China National Silk Museum (NSM) is a young museum. The museum has many galleries, including the Silk Road Gallery, the Sericulture Gallery, the Silk Weaving Gallery, the Conservation Gallery, the Fashion Gallery and more.

The Silk Road Gallery presents the history of silk in China. The Silk Weaving Gallery showcases China's sericulture and silk craftsmanship, which was listed on UNESCO's Intangible Culture Heritage List in 2009. There is also a sericulture house and a mulberry garden in the museum.

To promote scientific research, identification, protection and conservation of textile heritage in China, the NSM founded the Chinese Center for Textile Identification and Conservation in October, 2000. Since its establishment, the center has achieved fruitful results in textile analysis and examination, conservation and protection, production and craftsmanship, information gathering and research. Its work provides support for Chinese and international museums in the area of conservation and protection of cultural relics.

The Conservation Gallery features a textile conservation workshop and a display area, presenting exhibitions on conservational works.

The Fashion Gallery at the NSM showcases the fashion evolution in China and the West, hosting a series of temporary and special exhibitions. In 2016, *A World of Silks: International Silk Art Exhibition* was hosted at the NSM, featuring a rich collection of silk exhibits from South Korea, Japan, Russia, Indonesia, India and European countries. In 2018, the museum presented *A World of Looms: Weaving Technology and Textile Arts in China and Beyond* to showcase looms and other textile products from Africa, the Americas, Europe and Asia.

Three years ago, the International Association for the Study of Silk Roads Textiles (IASSRT) was established. Over 30 institutions and renowned scholars from 17 countries have joined the organization. Since its establishment, the association has organized exhibitions and several conferences to promote academic researches into the Silk Road. The First IASSRT Symposium was hosted by the NSM in 2016, accompanied by seminars and fashion shows. The Second IASSRT Symposium was hosted in Lyon, France in 2017. Over 40 scholars participated in the event and shared diverse local silk cultures during the two-day seminars. In November 2018, the Third IASSRT Symposium was hosted in Buyeo, Korea, with over 100 participants attending the event. After two days of seminars, participants traveled to Seoul and visited several Korean institutions including the National Museum of Korea and the textile studios. The 4th IASSRT

Symposium will be hosted in September 2019 in Russia, jointly organized by the Institute of Nasledie (Stravropol) Ltd. and the State Hermitage Museum in St. Petersburg. The 5th IASSRT Symposium is tentatively scheduled to be hosted in Italy from November 5 to 15, 2020, jointly organized by the NSM and the University of Padova. The NSM welcomes more organizations and institutions to join the IASSRT.

Regarding the Alliance's future work plans, the NSM invites all members to participate in the project "Interactive World Map of Silk". The project aims to carry out comprehensive and systematic survey of textile resources along the Silk Road and have these resources digitalized and archived, so as to lay a solid foundation for international study on Silk Roads textiles. The NSM will host seminars in Spain on the program next year. More participants are welcomed to join in the project.

The IAMS will generate future work plans with members for the next five years. The NSM, on its part, will host a special exhibition *Life along the Silk Road: 13 Stories during the Great Era*, which is inspired by the book with the same title. The author Susan Whitfield retells the history of the Silk Road by recounting stories of soldiers, merchants, monks, people of different ethnicities, with different identities and living in different historical periods. The exhibition has three sections. The first section "Steppe Silk Road" tells the story of two clans. The second section "Desert and Oasis Silk Road" features rich content that reflects life at the time, showing costumes, culture, lifestyles, religions and burial rites of different people including bailiff at a courier station, a general, a Western merchant and Buddhist monks. The last section "Maritime Silk Road" focuses on telling stories of two characters. A myriad of exquisite silk garments found in a royal tomb of the daughter of a customs chief in Fuzhou reflects the artistic weaving techniques in the Southern Song dynasty. Through exploring the sweet and sour life of the owner of the shipwreck Nanhai No.1, the spectacle of maritime trade will be reflected.

To accompany the exhibition, the NSM will host a curator's forum "Collaborations on the Silk Road Exhibitions". Curators from different museums will gather to discuss collaborations on the Silk Road exhibitions, exchange experience in curating the Silk Road exhibitions and

report results of their academic researches. In May 2019, the NSM plans to hold the first "Biennale of Natural Dyes" and accompanying seminars, introducing typical dyes, dying techniques and the color cultures around the world.

In regards to future work plans for the IAMS, we suggest the Alliance set up special committees to lead works in areas such as exhibitions, conservation and training. Located in Hangzhou, the China National Silk Museum, with beautiful environment and well-equipped infrastructure, will be supportive in organizing activities, such as training, in the future.

Conference Papers

Dr. Zhao Feng

Vice President, International Alliance of Museums of the Silk Road

Director, China National Silk Museum

Profile:

Zhao Feng is the director of the China National Silk Museum (NSM) in Hangzhou and the president of the International Association for the Study of Silk Roads Textiles (IASSRT).

During his career at the NSM since 1991, he studied the history of textiles at the China Textile University (Donghua University nowadays) in Shanghai and got his PhD in 1997. He got the fellowship and did researches at the Metropolitan Museum of Art in New York from Nov. 1997 to Oct. 1998, at the Royal Ontario Museum in Toronto for two months in 1999, and at the British Museum in London for half a year in 2006. In 2000, he founded and became the director of the Chinese Center for Textile Identification and Conservation, which is now the Key Scientific Research Base of Textile Conservation of State Administration of Cultural Heritage of China.

Since 1992, he has published more than 20 academic books and 100 research articles, including *The General History of Chinese Silk*, editor in chief, National Publication Award, 2007; *Chinese Silks*, editor in chief for the Chinese version, the R.L. Shep Ethnic Textiles Book Award for 2012; and *A Comprehensive Research on Textiles from Dunhuang* in UK's collections and French collections, 2007-now.

Fujian Museum

Wu Zhiyue

Vice President, International Alliance of Museums of the Silk Road

Director, Fujian Museum

Located at the West Lake Park in Fuzhou city, Fujian Museum is the only six-in-one comprehensive provincial museum complex in China, combined with the Natural Science Center, the Jicuiyuan Gallery, the Institute of Archaeology, the Cultural Relics Conservation Center and the National Underwater Archeology Research Base. The museum has won excellence of the most innovative, inspirational and awarded project in the field of museums, heritage and conservation in 2016. In 2015, as the world's only museum representative, Fujian Museum participated in the "Belt and Road" seminar held during the 70th anniversary of the UN. Besides, it is the only museum winning gold award in consecutive years in the Cross-Strait Cultural Industries Fair. In 2015, Fujian Museum was awarded the honorary title of "The Most Innovative Museum in China" by the Chinese Museums Association.

Fujian Museum has a collection of more than 280,000 objects. It covers the Maritime Silk Road, overseas Chinese, the Red Revolution and many other categories. The permanent exhibition *The Splendid Civilization of Ancient Fujian* covers an area of 1,400 square meters. A total of 503 pieces of relics are on display, including 12 screens by Shi Tao and "*To My Wife*" by Lin Juemin. The exhibition won the "Best Content Design Award" at the Ninth National Top Ten Museum Exhibitions.

Since 2010, the Fujian Museum had spent three years building a joint exhibition of Chinese Maritime Silk Road cultural relics – *Splendor of the Maritime Silk Road*. It has so far been exhibited in 24 cities in 11 provinces in China and 23 cities in 20 countries abroad. The exhibition won the title "National Top Ten Museum Exhibitions" and was praised by the Ministry of Foreign Affairs. The exhibition *The Overseas Chinese – the Spirit of Dedication* was curated in response to the theme exhibition project launched by the National Cultural Heritage Administration to promote excellent traditional culture and cultivate socialist core values. Fujian has raised 18.6 million overseas Chinese. Chen Jiageng, who was honored by Chairman Mao as "the flag of overseas Chinese, a banner of national glory", was born in Fujian. In 2018, the museum planed and presented a similar exhibition featuring overseas Chinese, namely *Following the Footsteps of Great Overseas Chinese Exhibition*.

In terms of research, the Fujian Museum implements "Ten Major Issues", "Five-Year Plan" and "Million Investment" to encourage academic research and publication. In terms of innovation in public services, the "200" project are held to regularly serve 100 higher education institutions and 100 communities each year. Fujian Museum has created "museum on paper", "museum on the airplane", "museum on the subway" and online museum. An airport museum covering 2,000 square meters is under construction.

Fujian Museum has four underwater cultural heritage protection projects underway across the country. In Kenya and the Xisha Islands, underwater archaeological projects in cooperation with the National Museum of China have been carrying out for more than 20 years. Furthermore, new finds were discovered in the underwater archaeological site in Pingtan.

Mr. Wu Zhiyue

Vice President, International Alliance of Museums of the Silk Road
Director, Fujian Museum

Profile:

Wu Zhiyue is a Research Fellow in the culture and museum field recognized and sponsored by China's State Council. He is the Deputy Director of Fujian Provincial Cultural Heritage Administration, Director of Fujian Museum, Director of the Special Committee of Museums of the Silk Road of Chinese Museums Association and Executive Director of Chinese Museums Association. He was shortlisted in the top 100 "Person of Chinese Cultural Management" in 2014 and was awarded the title of "Advanced Worker of National Cultural System" in 2015. He also serves in the jury for the senior academic titles awarding held by the Ministry of Culture and Tourism and Chinese museums, the China National Arts Fund, National Top Ten Museum Exhibitions, Design and Construction Qualification of Chinese museums, as well as the award for Excellent Academic Achievements in Chinese Museology Area.

Practice and Exploration of Cultural Exchanges with Museums along the Belt and Road: Xi'an Tang West Market Museum

Wang Bin

Vice President, International Alliance of Museums of the Silk Road

Director, Xi'an Tang West Market Museum

The Xi'an Tang West Market Museum (hereinafter referred to as TWMM) is a young, private museum as well as the first private on-the-site museum in China. The museum, invested by Tang West Market Cultural Industries Investment Group, is an exploration of private

capital participating in cultural heritage protection and museum operation. It is an important component and the cultural core of the Group's cultural projects. The Tang West Market National Cultural Industry Demonstration Base covers an area of 333,333 square meters, with a construction area of 1,280,000 square meters, and a total investment of RMB 8 billion yuan. The museum occupies an area of 13,333 square meters with a construction area of 35,000 square meters. Since its opening on April 7, 2010, the museum has been adhering to social welfare and cultural industry. It receives more than 600,000 audiences every year, with a total of more than 5 million audiences. The museum carries out social education programs, exhibitions and scientific researches, in accordance with national professional standards.

I. To continuously strengthen the theme of the Silk Road and to enrich its cultural connotation

The TWMM is located right on the original site of the West Market of Chang'an, the capital of Tang dynasty with 1,400 years' history. As an on-the-site museum, the exhibitions are mainly themed on the Silk Road. The permanent exhibition *A Thriving Trade Center at the Starting Point of the Silk Road* focuses on the narration of history. The thematic exhibition *Ancient Coins from the Silk Road* exhibits more than 1,400 ancient coins from 47 countries and tells the local customs and histories of their time and culture. The museum also held a special exhibition with its silk collections, *The Splendid Silk Road – A Selective Exhibition of the Silk Collection at the Tang West Market Museum*. Displays were either unearthed from the West Market, donated by the museum's founder or acquired through donations and auctions. The *Collection of Classics on the Silk Road – Refined Exhibition at Xi'an Tang West Market Museum* interprets the Silk Road culture with 26,975 relics which are mainly ceramics, porcelains and gold and silver wares. Another exhibition called *Splendid Silks and Flourishing Western Cultures Once along the Silk Road* introduced cultural exchanges along the Silk Road through the patterns on silk.

The museum has held 76 temporary exhibitions mainly featuring the Silk Road, such as a Silk Road diplomatic gift exchange exhibition hosted in cooperation with the International

Friendship Museum and a facsimile painting exhibition on Buddhist cave mural art jointly held with Shanghai East Dunhuang Zen Art Center. *History of the Great Silk Road – Shadow Theatre of Shaanxi Province* presents the cultural exchange features of the Silk Road by telling the stories of Wang Zhaojun, Zhang Qian and *Journey to the West*.

Educational activities at the museum also follow the Silk Road theme. Since the West Market is a historical trade center, the museum organized a children's flea market to improve their interpersonal, math and language skills. The event followed the ritualized opening and closing ceremony and sincere transactions of the Tang West Market at that time, thus were widely welcomed. A hands-on leather-silhouette activity accompanying the theme exhibition has been warmly received by domestic and foreign audiences. Lectures held inside and outside the museum also focused on the Silk Road stories and spirit. When visiting local communities and universities, lecturers dressed in Tang attires to explain the clothing, food, living and traveling of the Tang people. From 2015 to 2018, the museum organized student museum guide competitions with local universities. In 2018, the museum held a museum guide training course for children. Similar activities with focus on the Silk Road all received positive feedbacks.

The museum's cultural sector also extended the Silk Road theme. The Silk Road Cultural Experience Center of the museum consists of three sections: the exhibition section, the experience section and the research section, which aims to enable the audience to understand the ancient Silk Road culture as well as silk's appearance in historical and cultural elements and its application in modern life. Traditional handicraft experience activities were offered in *Hands-on Experience of the Silk Road Crafts*, and the products can also be sold at the museum.

II. Promoting museum cooperation to enlarge our circle of friends

Since the Belt and Road Initiative was proposed in 2013, the TWMM has been actively engaged in promoting cooperation with museums along the Silk Road. The museum has signed cooperation agreements with museums from Kyrgyzstan, Uzbekistan, Mongolia, Kazakhstan, Ukraine, etc. Twenty-two museums of 16 countries have become sister museums with us.

Meanwhile, the TWMM seeks further exhibition cooperation with other museums. In

2014, *History of the Great Silk Road – Shadow Theatre of Shaanxi Province* was launched at the State History Museum of Kyrgyzstan, and the exhibition about the material culture of Kirghiz in the 19th and 20th centuries was introduced to the TWMM. In 2015, the same exhibition on Shaanxi leather-silhouette was held at the Central State Museum of the Republic of Kazakhstan, and in turn in 2016, the TWMM launched *The World Famous Chocolate Exhibition of Nikolya* from Kazakhstan, which was also presented in other provinces such as Ningxia and Jilin and generated great social influence and benefit. In 2018, *Early Nomadic Culture on the Eurasian Steppe – Kazakh Culture Relics Exhibition* was hosted in Xi'an. It was the first time the Central State Museum of the Republic of Kazakhstan presented an exhibition in China.

The TWMM has also helped other museums or institutions to establish connections. For example, communication and cooperation between the Frunze Museum, Kyrgyzstan and the Xi'an Eighth Route Army Office Museum, Kulob Republican Local Lore Museum Complex and Shaanxi Provincial Institute of Cultural Heritage were both promoted by the TWMM.

The museum has actively built a platform to promote people-to-people exchange. In cooperation with the Shaanxi Provincial Women's Federation, Xi'an's first "Silk Road Women's Home" was established at the museum, focusing on people-to-people exchanges with female compatriots along the Silk Road. On September 6, 2016, the TWMM led the establishment of the Silk Road International Museum Alliance and held the first alliance conference. The alliance currently has a total of 66 member museums from 17 countries, of which 22 are international and 44 are in the country.

In the future, the TWMM will work fully in line with the unified deployment of the IAMS and work actively in accordance with the Alliance's planning, enhancing cooperation with other museums, enlarging the circle of friends, and building platforms for cultural exchanges. Finally, it is hoped that the Alliance would mobilize all resources and prioritize focus on the development of research, exhibition, education as well as cultural and creative centers. In addition, we should actively promote multidiscipline convergence in the fields of cultural relics, digitalization and the internet, creating new platform for new forms of display and exchange.

Ms. Wang Bin

Vice President, International Alliance of Museums of the Silk Road

Director, Xi'an Tang West Market Museum

Educational Background:

MA in History

Research Fellow

Professional Experience:

Wang worked as a research fellow and the Deputy Director at Shaanxi History Museum. She has been devoted to museum industry since 1981 and is currently the director of Xi'an Tang West Market Museum and Vice Chairman of Tang West Market Group. Besides, Ms. Wang is the Chairman of the Silk Road International Museum Alliance, a council member of China Cultural Relics Academy and a specialist of National Cultural Heritage Administration.

Academic Achievements:

As a researcher in History, Wang is the author of many books such as *Interpretation of National Treasure, The Glory and Dream of Shaanxi, Shaanxi History Museum, Tang West Market in History, Xi'an Tang West Market Museum*, etc. Meanwhile, she has achieved a lot in the study of women's clothing in Tang dynasty and in the practice of private museum theories.

Closing Speech ▪

闭幕致辞

Closing Speech at the First Conference of the International Alliance of Museums of the Silk Road

Wang Chunfa

President, International Alliance of Museums of the Silk Road
Director, National Museum of China

With the extensive participation and joint efforts of representatives from the IAMS members, during the past one and a half days of meeting, we witnessed the official launch of the IAMS website, discussed and passed the Statutes of the International Alliance of Museums of the Silk Road, adopted four new international Vice-President units, jointly signed the Framework Agreement on IAMS Exhibition Cooperation and the Memorandum on the IAMS First Conference, determined the time and place for the next IAMS Conference and successfully completed the established procedures.

The conference is open, pragmatic and fruitful. Representatives shared their achievements and experience on the development of national museums, put forward thoughts and suggestions and discussed approaches and methods to embrace the opportunities and challenges brought by the in-depth development of the world's multi-polarization, economic globalization, social informatization and cultural diversity.

In the new era, we share a common future. It is gratifying that we have achieved a consensus on practicing the Silk Road Spirit featuring peace and cooperation, openness and inclusiveness, and mutual learning and mutual benefit in the museum field. It is believed that in the current world economic situation, to explore the development of theme exhibitions, information sharing, joint research, personnel exchanges and training by the IAMS in the field of cultural heritage will promote the international cooperation between museums in countries and regions along the Silk Road. Thus, I would like to make a few suggestions on the future development of the IAMS:

First, to promote exhibition cooperation and advance exchanges and mutual learning among civilizations. We shall further enhance communication and coordination within the alliance. Members of the IAMS shall launch at least one joint exhibition or tour exhibition each year. The exhibition will be jointly curated by relevant members to showcase diverse civilizations, bring the rich collections of cultural relics to life in museums of the countries and regions along the Silk Road, continue to increase the public's attention and participation in cross-regional and cross-cultural exchanges and cooperation, deepen the people-to-people bond and strengthen exchanges and mutual learning among world civilizations. Academic forums shall be held during exhibitions and tour exhibitions to respond in a timely manner to the key points, difficulties and hot topics shared by the alliance members.

Second, to strengthen personnel exchanges and build synergies. Talent is at the core of meeting future challenges. All members shall take advantage of the IAMS platform to jointly promote the in-depth development of talent exchanges and cooperation, jointly develop professional talent training and academic exchanges in the fields of management, exhibition, archaeology, heritage conservation and research and achieve normalization and institutionalization of professionals' exchange visits. The National Museum of China is willing to carry out exchanges, cooperation and training programs, and each year, to exchange three to five young and seasoned experts and scholars with each IAMS member. I suggest that from 2019, members of the alliance shall conduct at least one seminar or exchange program annually in various fields and on different themes. The theme of 2019 is "New Era and Strategic Development", which will be hosted by the National Museum of China. In the future, all member units are welcome to undertake related themed activities.

Third, to carry out conservation of cultural relics and archaeological cooperation and jointly protect human cultural heritage. Museums around the world differ in many aspects such as conservation and archaeological policies and regulations, historical evolution as well as scientific and technological conditions. Thus, cooperation among alliance members should facilitate mutual learning and complement each other's advantages. As a future step, IAMS members should work together to explore a joint mechanism for scientific excavation, conservation and restoration of cultural relics, especially the exchanges and mutual learning of cultural relics conservation technologies in certain areas; to improve professional skills and operational ability and strengthen scientific excavation and preventive conservation of cultural relics; to jointly combat the smuggling and illegal trafficking of antiques in order to protect the cultural heritage shared by all mankind. Basic researches such as the human origins tracing project and the human migration map should act as important directions for the study of the cultural relevance of countries and regions along the Silk Road, and joint archaeology should be actively carried out .

Fourth, to promote the application of new technologies and the construction of smart museums and share innovative development experience. In the ever-changing information society, technological innovation has become a new engine for the future development of museums. At present, the National Museum of China is making every effort to promote the construction of the "Smart NMC". We are willing to work with IAMS members to discuss new directions for the development of smart museums, give each other priority in providing intelligence and technical equipment support and make use of new technologies' positive function in museum collection preservation, exhibition display and public education, such as big data, cloud computing, 3D printing, AR, etc. We should take full advantage of the IAMS website to strengthen the digitization and informatization of member museums' collections, unblock the channels for resource sharing and information release and propel the sustainable and high-quality development of all members.

Fifth, to strengthen the cooperation on cultural and creative development, bring cultural relics to life and realize the functional transformation of cultural relics. In the global context of "museum fever", cultural and creative products that integrate traditional and fashionable elements are becoming increasingly popular, serving as an important carrier for conveying knowledge of cultural relics, expressing aesthetic values and bringing audience closer to museums. The National Museum of China attaches great importance to the research and development of cultural and creative products. We have launched a number of favorable products. Alliance members shall rely on their featured collections to strengthen cooperation on IP authorization, joint research and development of cultural and creative products and give priority to alliance members for authorization, promotion and sales to enhance the cultural significance and intellectual value of cultural heritages. Based on the IAMS platform and member museums' collections, cultural exchanges and other activities, such as fashion weeks, sports festivals, comic conventions, music festivals and film festivals could also be planned and implemented.

Ideas lead to prosperity. Through the IAMS platform, we must continuously strengthen the mechanisms, clarify the goals and solidify the foundation for cooperation. At the same time, we are also aware of the importance of actively adapting to the new situation and changes, accelerating reform and innovation, stimulating the vitality of the museums' sustainable development and striving to promote the construction of a human community with a shared future.

Ladies and gentlemen, friends! "Someday, with my sail piercing the clouds; I will mount the wind, break the waves, and traverse the vast, rolling sea." In the new era, at a new start and with a new mission, we shall be brave to undertake responsibilities, move forward unswervingly, take concrete actions to promote continuous new progress in the alliance work and inject strong impetus into building a human community with a shared future

We will always remember our gathering in Fuzhou! In concluding, I would like to once again extend my thanks to all IAMS members for your efforts in preparing and organizing this conference. In 2020, we look forward to meeting you again in Beijing!

Achievements ■

论坛成果

Achievement 1：

(Translation for Reference)

Memorandum on the IAMS First Executive Council Meeting

Under the framework of the Statutes of the International Alliance of Museums of the Silk Road (IAMS), the first meeting of the Executive Council of the IAMS is held in Fuzhou, China, on November 24, 2018, which is attended by the President, Vice Presidents and Secretary General of the IAMS. Consensus has been reached as following:

I. After discussion among members, it is agreed that four new international Vice-President units will join the Executive Council. The list is as follows:

A. National Museum of Myanmar (Yangon)

B. National Museum of the Republic of Kazakhstan

C. National Museum of History of Azerbaijan

D. National Museum in Belgrade, Serbia

II. The IAMS Second Conference will be held at the National Museum of China in Beijing in November 2020.

The IAMS Conference, which is held every two years thereafter, shall be chaired alternately by members who are capable of holding it. As for the exact schedule and agenda, the IAMS Secretariat shall inform the members after negotiations among the members.

Achievement 2:

Memorandum on the IAMS
First Conference

Under the framework of the Statutes of the International Alliance of Museums of the Silk Road (IAMS), the IAMS First Conference is held on 24 to 25 November 2018 in Fuzhou, China. Altogether 17 members from 12 countries in Asia, Europe and Africa attend the Conference, at which the members have discussed the Statutes and future cooperation among other affairs, and reached the following consensus:

I. The IAMS members confirm that the IAMS is a non-governmental, non-profit and open international cooperation mechanism and communication platform in the field of museums for countries and regions along the Silk Road. All the IAMS members agree that they shall uphold the Silk Road Spirit that stresses peaceful cooperation, openness and inclusiveness, mutual learning and mutual benefit to carry out cooperation and exchanges in multiple aspects.

II. The IAMS members have, after discussion, endorsed the Statutes of the International Alliance of Museums of the Silk Road and agreed to observe the Statutes, and to foster cooperation and exchanges among museums in countries and regions along the Silk Road.

III. The members have signed the Framework Agreement on IAMS Exhibition Cooperation, and will jointly participate in the exhibitions series on the theme of "Exchanges and Mutual Learning between Civilizations", which is to be held at the National Museum of China.

IV. The IAMS website is launched. The National Museum of China shall be responsible for its operation by timely updating the webpage and releasing cooperation results.

V. After discussion among members, it is agreed that four new international Vice-President units will join the Executive Council. The list is as follows:

A. National Museum of Myanmar (Yangon)

B. National Museum of the Republic of Kazakhstan

C. National Museum of History of Azerbaijan

D. National Museum in Belgrade, Serbia

VI. The IAMS Second Conference shall be held at the National Museum of China in Beijing in November 2020. The IAMS Conference, which is held every two years thereafter, is chaired alternately by members who are capable of holding it. As for the exact schedule and agenda, the IAMS Secretariat shall inform the members after negotiations among the members.

Signed by representatives to the IAMS First Conference:

Wang Chunfa, Director of the National Museum of China

An Laishun, Secretary General of the Chinese Museums Association

Zhao Feng, Director of the China National Silk Museum

Wu Zhiyue, Director of the Fujian Museum, China

Wang Bin, Director of the Xi'an Tang West
Market Museum, China

Naila Valikhanova, Director of the National
Museum of History of Azerbaijan

Satubaldin Abay Karemtaevich, Deputy Director
of the National Museum of the Republic of
Kazakhstan

Khamit Aitkul, Head of Archaeological Centre
of the Central State Museum of the Republic
of Kazakhstan

Kong Vireak, Director of the National
Museum of Cambodia

Phetmalayvanh Keobounma, Director of the
Lao National Museum

Budbayar Ishgen, Head of Policy Planning
and Administration Division of the National
Museum of Mongolia

Daw Nang Lao Ngin, Director of the National
Museum of Myanmar (Yangon)

Orit Shamir, Head of the Department of Museums and Exhibits, Israel Antiquities Authority

Omar Idtnaine, Program Manager of the Azart Association, Morocco

Luda Tolkacheva, Head of the Department of Archeology, Numismatics and Weapon, National Historical Museum of the Republic of Belarus

Zvezdana Dode, Senior Researcher of the Institute of Nasledie (Stravropol) Ltd.

Bojana Borić Brešković, Director of the National Museum in Belgrade, Republic of Serbia

25 November 2018
Fuzhou, China

Achievement 3:

Statutes of the International Alliance of Museums of the Silk Road

I. General Provisions

The International Alliance of Museums of the Silk Road (IAMS) is a non-governmental, non-profit and open international cooperation mechanism and communication platform in the field of museums for countries and regions along the Silk Road. The IAMS advocates internationalization, openness and democracy. Its members should respect each other's traditional customs and comply with laws and regulations.

II. Mission

The IAMS is committed to actively exploring thematic exhibitions, information sharing, joint research, professional exchanges and personnel training in the field of cultural heritage in countries and regions along the Silk Road, promoting international cooperation among museums in countries and regions along the Silk Road, and strengthening contact and cooperation with international institutions and organizations related to these museums. It is also dedicated to improving the society's attention to and participation in cross-cultural exchanges and cooperation, thus forging a bond of friendship for all people on the Silk Road.

Its mission includes:

A. Enhancing mutual understanding and friendships by implementing cooperation and exchanges in museum-related services such as exhibitions, professionals and cultural heritage protection;

B. Exploring the feasibility of an information sharing website of the IAMS in countries and regions along the Silk Road through cooperation in the digital field;

C. Spreading extensively to the world the rich histories and cultures of countries and regions along the Silk Road through regular IAMS Conferences;

D. Encouraging members to cooperate in the following areas:

1. Holding the IAMS Conference on a regular basis;

2. Presenting joint exhibitions to accompany the IAMS Conference;

3. Organizing museum directors' forums to accompany the IAMS Conference;

4. Having exhibition exchanges among IAMS members;

5. Having professional exchanges and trainings among IAMS members;

6. Having exchanges and cooperation in the field of cultural heritage protection among IAMS members;

7. Carrying out cooperation in digitization and exploring the feasibility of an information sharing website of the IAMS in countries and regions along the Silk Road; and

8. Carrying out other museum-related exchanges and cooperation.

III. Members

The IAMS now has 157 members, including 47 international institutions and 110 Chinese institutions.

A. Member application and withdrawal procedures

In the spirit of openness, the IAMS is growing its members.

The member admission procedures are as follows:

1. Submitting an application for membership;

2. Discussed and approved by the Executive Council; and

3. A membership certificate issued by the Secretariat.

The withdrawal of a member from the IAMS shall be notified to the Secretariat in written form. The membership shall be automatically cancelled if a member fails to participate in activities of the IAMS for five consecutive years.

B. Membership eligibility

1. Supporting the initiative of establishing the IAMS and the Statutes;

2. Having the will to join the IAMS;

3. Having a certain impact in the museum circle; and

4. Obeying the leadership of the IAMS and actively participating in activities organized by the IAMS.

C. Rights of members

1. Sharing resources of the IAMS in accordance with the Statutes and related agreements;

2. Organizing or supporting activities in the name of the IAMS with the approval from the Executive Council; and

3. Joining or withdrawing from the IAMS voluntarily.

D. Obligations of members

1. Complying with the Statutes, rules and regulations, and implementing resolutions of the IAMS;

2. Actively participating in activities organized by the IAMS, providing resource support, and striving to contribute to the building and development of the IAMS;

3. Safeguarding the interests and legitimate rights of the IAMS; and

4. Receiving supervision and inspection of the IAMS regarding projects that are applied for or undertaken in the name of the IAMS, and performing the contract as agreed.

IV. Organization

The organization consists of the Executive Council and the Secretariat.

A. Executive Council

The Executive Council consists of the President, Secretary General and Vice Presidents. Now it has ten members and the total number of members shall not exceed 21.

1. Members of the Executive Council are as follows:

a) President - Director of the National Museum of China

b) Secretary General - Deputy Director of the National Museum of China

c) Vice President - Secretary General of the Chinese Museums Association

d) Vice President - Director of the China National Silk Museum

e) Vice President - Director of the Fujian Museum

f) Vice President - Director of the Tang West Market Museum

g) Vice President - Director of the National Museum of Myanmar (Yangon)

h) Vice President - Director of the National Museum of the Republic of Kazakhstan

i) Vice President - Director of the National Museum of History of Azerbaijan

j) Vice President - Director of the National Museum in Belgrade, Serbia

2. Tenure

If a member of the Executive Council is no longer in the position of his/her unit due to retirement or resignation, and is replaced by another person, the name of the successor shall be notified to the Secretariat in time and confirmed by the Executive Council Meeting.

3. President's authority

The President has the right to convene the Executive Council Meeting.

4. President's responsibility

The President is responsible for notifying the members of the decisions made at the Executive Council Meeting.

5. Secretary General's duties

a) Managing daily work of the Secretariat and organizing the implementation of the annual work plan; and

b) Handling other daily tasks.

B. Secretariat

The Secretariat is based at the National Museum of China (located at the east side of the Tiananmen Square, Beijing, China)

1. Head of the General Office of the Secretariat - Head of the International Department of the National Museum of China

2. Deputy Head of the General Office of the Secretariat - Deputy Secretary General of the Chinese Museums Association

3. Members of the Secretariat - Staff of the National Museum of China

C. Liaison officer

Each member shall appoint a liaison officer responsible for liaison with the Secretariat.

V. Conference and Meeting

A. The IAMS Conference is held every two years. The aim is to promote the development of and cooperation among museums in countries and regions along the Silk Road, and to effectively carry out exchanges and cooperation among countries and regions along the Silk Road.

B. The Executive Council Meeting shall be convened at least once a year by the Secretariat, and participated in by the Executive Council members. The Meeting can be held with the presence of more than half of the Executive Council members, and any resolution shall come into force upon being adopted at the Meeting.

C. The IAMS First Conference and First Executive Council Meeting were held in November 2018 in Fujian, China to discuss and adopt the Statutes.

VI. Funds

The National Museum of China is responsible for the daily expenses of the IAMS Secretariat. It encourages the members to actively carry out activities. The specific activities are funded by the participating units.

VII. Dispute Resolution

Any dispute shall be handled through friendly negotiation. If the negotiation fails, the dispute shall be submitted to a third-party arbitral institution for arbitration, and the arbitration award shall be final and binding on all parties to the dispute.

VIII. Supplementary Provisions

The Statutes have been voted on and endorsed at the First IAMS Conference held on 24

November 2018 and shall take effect immediately. The right of interpretation and revision of the Statutes shall be vested in the Executive Council.

24 November 2018

Achievement 4:

Framework Agreement on IAMS Exhibition Cooperation

The International Alliance of Museums of the Silk Road (IAMS) is a non-governmental, non-profit, open international cooperation mechanism and communication platform in the field of museums for countries and regions along the Silk Road.

To fully demonstrate diversity and globalization in cooperation and exchanges, the National Museum of China, as the President unit of the IAMS, will partner with 17 national museums worldwide to host an exhibition in Beijing at the beginning of 2019 on the theme of "Exchanges and Mutual Learning among Civilizations". The exhibition aims to unfold, through antiquities, the history of exchanges and communication in trade, belief, science and technology, lifestyle, culture and art among countries along the Silk Road. In this way, it will present the dialogue and integration among civilizations and provide historical examples for exchanges, mutual learning and win-win cooperation among these civilizations under the Belt and Road framework.

On the occasion of the IAMS First Conference and under the framework of the IAMS Statues, we, 17 institutions from 12 countries, all agree to participate in the exhibition Exchanges and Mutual Learning among Civilizations to achieve the Silk Road Spirit of peaceful cooperation, openness and inclusiveness, mutual learning and mutual benefit.

Signed by representatives to the IAMS First Conference:

Wang Chunfa, Director of the National Museum of China

An Laishun, Secretary General of the Chinese Museums Association

Zhao Feng, Director of the China National Silk Museum

Wu Zhiyue, Director of the Fujian Museum, China

Wang Bin, Director of the Xi'anTang West Market Museum, China

Naila Valikhanova, Director of the National Museum of History of Azerbaijan

Satubaldin Abay Karemtaevich, Deputy Director of the National Museum of the Republic of Kazakhstan

Khamit Aitkul, Head of Archaeological Centre of the Central State Museum of the Republic of Kazakhstan

Kong Vireak, Director of the National
Museum of Cambodia

Phetmalayvanh Keobounma, Director of the
Lao National Museum

Budbayar Ishgen, Head of Policy Planning
and Administration Division of the National
Museum of Mongolia

Daw Nang Lao Ngin, Director of the National
Museum of Myanmar (Yangon)

Orit Shamir, Head of the Department of
Museums and Exhibits, Israel Antiquities Authority

Omar Idtnaine, Program Manager of the
Azart Association, Morocco

Archaeology Luda Tolkacheva, Head of the
Department of Archaeology, Numismatics and
Weapon, National Historical Museum of the
Republic of Belarus

Zvezdana Dode, Senior Researcher of the
Institute of Nasledie (Stravropol) Ltd.

Bojana Borić Brešković, Director of the
National Museum in Belgrade, Republic of
Serbia

24 November 2018
Fuzhou, China

Appendix ■
附录

Membership List of the International Alliance of Museums of the Silk Road

The IAMS has a total of 157 members (as of November, 2018), including 47 international members and 110 Chinese members.

International Members

Asia

National Museum of History of Azerbaijan

Pakistan Museum of Natural History

The Palestinian Museum

National Museum of the Republic of Kazakhstan

Central State Museum of the Republic of Kazakhstan

Korea National University of Cultural Heritage

State History Museum of Kyrgyzstan

Frunze Museum

National Museum of Cambodia

Lao National Museum

National Museum of Mongolia

National Museum of Myanmar (Yangon)

National Museum of Tajikistan

Museum Complex of Kulob, Republic of Tajikistan

Queen Sirikit Museum of Textiles

State Museum of the History of Uzbekistan

Bukhara Museum

Institute of Archaeology, Academy of Sciences of the Republic of Uzbekistan

National Museum of Yemen

Israel Antiquities Authority

Indian Institute of World Culture

The Traditional Textile Arts Society of South East Asia (TTASSEA)

Africa

Médéa Museum, Algeria

National Museum of Ethiopia

Azart Association

Museum of Black Civilizations

National Museum of Tanzania

Europe

National Historical Museum of the Republic of Belarus

Danish National Research Foundation's Center for Textile Research

National Museum of Denmark

Max Planck Institute for the History of Science

State Historical Museum of Russia

State Hermitage Museum

State Museum of Oriental Art

Russian Museum of Ethnography

Institute of Nasledie (Stavropol) Ltd.

Institute of Ancient History and Archaeology of the Northern Caucasus

Textile Arts Museum

Swedish History Museum

National Museum in Belgrade, Serbia

Nikolya Chocolate Museum

University of Padova

International Dunhuang Project, British Library

The Needham Research Institute, Cambridge University

McDonald Institute for Archaeological Research, Cambridge University

America

America Goddess Art Museum

Bryant University

Chinese Members

Beijing

National Museum of China

Chinese Museums Association

The Palace Museum

Capital Museum

Center for Research on Ancient Chinese History, Peking University

China Customs Museum

Chinese Businessmen Museum

China Red Sandalwood Museum

Institute for the History of Natural Sciences, Chinese Academy of Sciences

Tianjin

Tianjin Museum

Tianjin Agarwood Art Museum

Hebei

Hebei Museum

Hebei Dashengtang Ancient Pottery Museum

Hengshui Museum of Inside Painting Art

Sun Yingzhou Memorial Museum

Shanxi

Datong Museum

Linfen Wood-Block New Year Painting Museum

Inner Mongolia

Inner Mongolia Museum

Hohhot Museum

Inner Mongolia Mingbo Steppes Culture Museum

Liaoning

Liaoning Provincial Museum

Lushun Museum

Jilin

Jilin Provincial Museum

Heilongjiang

Museum of Heilongjiang Province

Shanghai

Shanghai Museum

China Maritime Museum

Shanghai Shihua Art Gallery

Liuli China Museum

College of Fashion and Design, Donghua University

Jiangsu

Nanjing Museum

Suzhou Museum

Yangzhou Museum

Zhenjiang Museum

Imperial Edict Museum, Xuzhou

Zhejiang

China National Silk Museum

Zhejiang Provincial Museum

Ningbo Museum

Shaoxing Yue Culture Museum

Collaborative Innovation Center for the Belt and Road Initiative, Zhejiang University

Anhui

Anhui Museum

Yuan Quan Hui Culture Folk Museum

Fujian

Fujian Museum

Fuzhou Museum

Quanzhou Museum

Tan Kah Kee Memorial Museum

Quanzhou Maritime Museum

Zhenmei History and Culture Museum

Xiamen Olympic Museum

Jiangxi

Jiangxi Provincial Museum

Shandong

Shandong Museum

Qingdao Museum

Henan

Henan Museum

Luoyang Museum

Museum of Baihe Studio Chao Family Book Collection, Luoyang

Zhengzhou Daxiang Ceramic Museum

Guangdong

Guangdong Museum

Guangzhou Museum

Maritime Silk Road Museum of Guangdong

Guangxi

Museum of Guangxi Zhuang Autonomous Region

Hainan

Hainan Museum

Chongqing

Chongqing China Three Gorges Museum

Chongqing Baolin Museum

Sichuan

Sichuan Museum

Chengdu Museum

Chengdu Shu Brocade and Embroidery Museum

Sichuan Museum of Jianchuan

Guizhou

Guizhou Provincial Museum

Yunnan

Yunnan Provincial Museum

Yunnan Nationalities Museum

Tibet

Tibet Museum

Shaanxi

Xi'an Tang West Market Museum

Shaanxi History Museum

Famen Temple Museum

Xi'an Museum

Shaanxi Han Tang Stone Sculpture Museum

Shaanxi Wanda Museum

Shaanxi Tang Sancai Art Museum

Guanzhong Folk Art Museum

Xi'an Tang Bronze Mirror Museum

Hanguangmen Site Museum of Xi'an Tang City Wall

Xi'an Yuanhaohuazang Museum

Xi'an Tile and Brick Museum

Daming Palace Site Museum

Xianyang Museum

ICOMOS International Conservation Center-Xi'an (IICC-X)

Gansu

Gansu Provincial Museum

Gansu Provincial Institute of Cultural Relics and Archaeology

Dunhuang Academy

Gansu Bingling Temple Cultural Relics Research Institute

Maijishan Grottoes Art Research Institute

Lanzhou Museum

Wuwei Museum

Zhangye Municipal Cultural Heritage Administration

Zhangye Ganzhou District Museum

Jiuquan Museum

Jiayuguan Great Wall Museum

Dunhuang Museum

Yangguan Museum

Tianshui Museum

Pingliang Museum

Qinghai

Qinghai Provincial Museum

Ningxia

Ningxia Hui Autonomous Region Museum

Shuidonggou Site Museum

Guyuan Museum of Ningxia

Xinjiang

Xinjiang Uygur Autonomous Region Museum

Turpan Museum

Yili Kazak Autonomous Prefecture Museum

Cultural Relics and Archaeology Institute of Xinjiang Uygur Autonomous Region

Hong Kong

Ming and Qing Furniture Museum, Hong Kong

Macau

Macau Chinese Art Exchange Promotion Association

Introductions of Participating Organizations

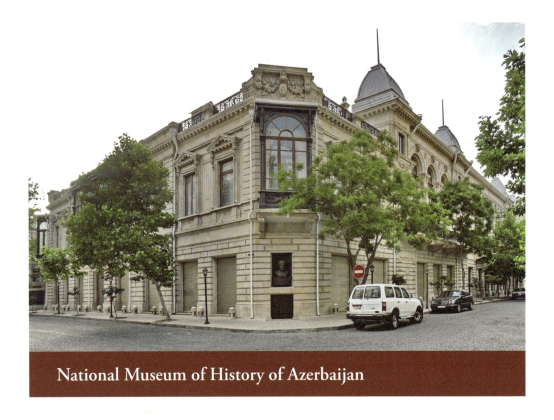

National Museum of History of Azerbaijan

The National Museum of History of Azerbaijan was founded on June 15th 1920. It became not only the first museum in the country, but also a scientific-educational center as well. From the very first day the Museum has been continuously expanding its collection by gathering and preserving artifacts from ancient ages until today. Currently, there are about 300 thousand artifacts in the museum's possession; also there are 11 funds (storages) and 6 academic departments, including archaeology, ethnography and numismatics as well as a restoration laboratory and a library.

The National Museum of History of Azerbaijan during its nearly 100 years of activity became an important academic and cultural center of historical research and place of preservation of cultural heritage. The National Museum of History of Azerbaijan is a scientific organization – part of the Azerbaijan National Academy of Science. The Museum publishes both informative materials and academic publications, such as albums, catalogs, books and monographs.

The National Museum of History of Azerbaijan has cooperated with different museums from around the world, including China, Turkey, Russia, Germany, Georgia, Uzbekistan, Kazakhstan, Italy, France, Poland, etc. The Museum has been involved in scientific conferences, symposiums and forums, information sharing, joint research, professional exchanges and personnel training in the field of cultural heritage. The Museum of History of Azerbaijan has conducted exhibitions in Germany, Great Britain, Norway, Vatican, Czech Republic and Kazakhstan and other countries.

A lot of people visit the museum every day and the museum team is making its efforts to attract visitors and familiarize them with the rich culture and history of Azerbaijan.

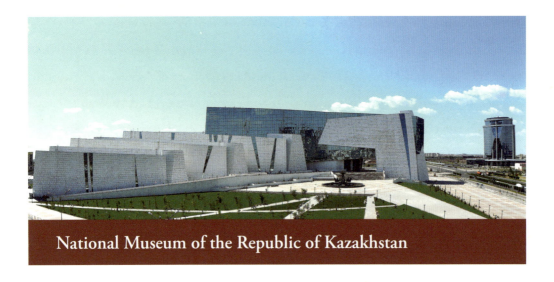

National Museum of the Republic of Kazakhstan

The National Museum of the Republic of Kazakhstan is a treasured component of the national history of Kazakhstan, an integral part of the culture and an unrivaled project of national importance. The Museum was founded on 2 July 2014 on the order of the President of Republic of Kazakhstan Nursultan Nazarbayev. The Museum's exhibition space ranges over an area of 14,000 square meters spread across 10 stationary halls. The total area of the Museum is 74,000 square meters, placing it in the top 10 largest museums in the world and making it ostensibly the largest museum in Central Asia. The atrium instantly captivates museum visitors with its surprising blend of light and sound. The exhibitions and permanent displays introduce you to the history and culture of Kazakhstan from ancient history right up to the modern day.

The National Museum's centerpiece multistory building touches the Astana skyline and blends in harmoniously with its surrounding on Independence Square. It is the final piece of the jigsaw comprising the Kazakh State Monument, the Palace of Independence, the Palace of Peace and Reconciliation, National University of the Arts and the Hazret Sultan Mosque.

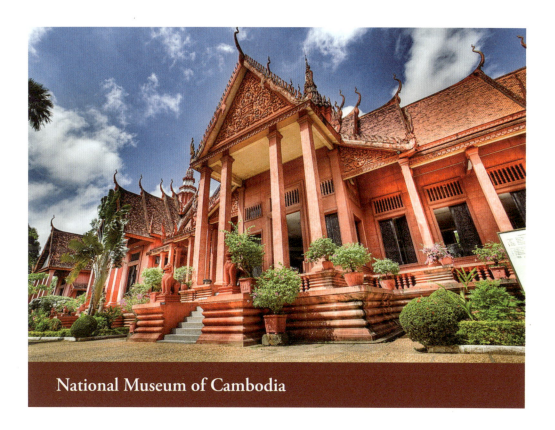

National Museum of Cambodia

Located in Phnom Penh, the capital of Cambodia, the National Museum of Cambodia is the leading museum of history and archaeology in the country. Founded 1917 to 1920, the museum houses one of the world's greatest collections of Khmer cultural heritage. It is mainly devoted to the protection, collection, publicity, restoration and inheritance of Cambodian cultural and artistic heritage. By visiting the museum collections, the audience can visually understand and experience the cultural heritage of Cambodia.

The total area of the museum is about 5200 square meters, including 2800 square meters of exhibition area. The museum building adopts the architectural style of herringbone roof, carved door and Khmer temple, which integrates the Khmer traditional building and French colonial style. It is one of the classic buildings in Phnom Penh.

At present, there are about 15,000 pieces of art works in the museum collection, and about 2000 pieces are displayed each time. The collection of the museum is rich and spans different

historical periods, including prehistoric, pre-Angkorian, Angkorian and post-Angkorian periods. There are four main categories of collections: stone, bronze, porcelain and wood. Stone objects are mainly stone sculptures of gods in Brahmanism and Buddhism, among which the inscriptions and architectural styles are also representative. Most of the collected bronzes are religious figures, ritual utensils and daily life utensils. Also, there are some cultural relics reflecting human civilization, such as pottery, porcelain and animal shaped containers. Most of the woodwork is benches for preaching, boxes, plates, looms and other carvings. In addition, the museum has a small collection of oil paintings, textiles, pictures and other archives.

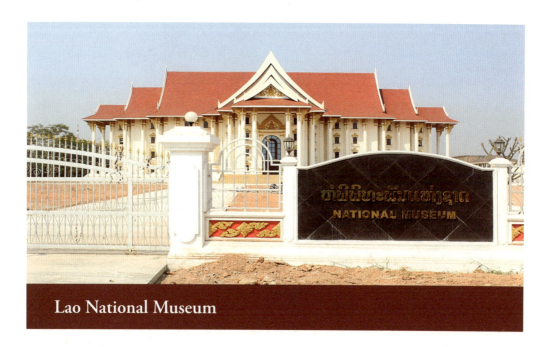

Lao National Museum

The Lao National Museum is a scientific research center and public institution dedicated to the study, preservation and promotion of the country's culture and history. The museum's old building was established in 1925, housed in one of the oldest remaining colonial buildings in Laos. In 1985, the place was named the Lao Revolutionary Museum. In 2000, the museum became the Lao National Museum. The museum's new building was built in 2017. The museum currently stores more than 28,000 registered artefacts and some 130,000 unregistered artefacts. Since 2000, the museum has welcomed thousands of domestic and overseas students and visitors every year.

National Museum of Myanmar (Yangon)

The National Museum of Myanmar (Yangon) was established in 1952 after Myanmar had gained its independence, by the newly formed Ministry of Culture. The exhibits were originally placed at the Jubilee Hall and were moved to Pansodan Road in 1970, then to the current location, 66/47 Pyay Road, Dagon Township, Yangon on 18th September, 1996. It is an imposing five storied building and the floor areas of exhibition are 194,800 square feet, with the mission to collect, display and preserve Myanmar cultural heritage objects.

The vision of the National Museum is to be the center for the people to learn Myanmar culture and civilization process so as to shape a better future by safeguarding the cultural heritage of Myanmar. According to this vision, the Museum displays a combination of themes of history, archaeology, arts and crafts, ethnology and other subjects. Over 4,000 pieces are displayed in 13 exhibition halls. The oldest exhibits are over 40 million years of age, before human beings evolved.

The National Museum of Myanmar (Yangon) is now carrying out five functions – collection, preservation and conservation of museum properties, research and publication, displaying (permanent and temporary), and public education.

Israel Antiquities Authority

The Israel Antiquities Authority (IAA) is an independent Israeli governmental authority in charge of the country's antiquities and antiquity sites, their excavation, preservation, conservation, study and publication thereof, enforcing the Antiquities Law 1978. It serves to maintain a balance between development needs and antiquities preservation.

Every year the IAA supports around 150 rescue excavations which yield many ancient artifacts. And in order to increase public awareness and interest in the country's archaeological heritage, the IAA monitors the archaeological displays and assists in updating them.

In Israel there are around 350 archaeological museums, exhibitions and outdoor exhibits around the country, some of which are decades old. Since the establishment of the State of Israel in 1948, archaeological museums and exhibitions have become very popular. Public interest in archaeology led to the creation of large collections, some of which are presented in museums. All the archaeological artifacts in these museums and exhibitions are registered at the IAA.

The IAA manages and lends out archaeological artifacts and encourages the establishment of exhibitions around the country: museums, national institutions, public institutions, research and educational institutions, national parks, visitor centers, schools and more.

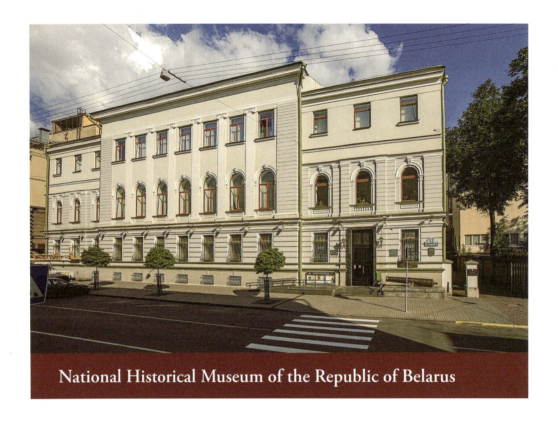

National Historical Museum of the Republic of Belarus

The National Historical Museum of the Republic of Belarus originates from a local history museum founded in 1919, but in 2009 it was renamed with present title. The museum has five branches: the Memorial House of First Congress of the Russian Social Democratic Labour Party, the Museum of the Theatrical and Musical Culture History, the Museum of Belarusian Cinema History, the Museum of Contemporary Belarusian Statehood, the Museum of Nature and Ecology. The collection of the National Historical Museum of the Republic of Belarus has more than 460 thousand units. Certain collections and objects are included in the State List of Historical and Cultural Heritage of the Republic of Belarus: treasure of Roman coins (1st–2nd centuries), set of silver waist plates (late 14th–early 15th centuries), Holy doors (18th century), Portrait of Jozef Prozor by unknown painter (late 18th–early 19th centuries). The museum works closely with private collectors. In 2008, on the basis of the museum, the State Catalogue of the Museum Collection of the Republic of Belarus was created. This catalogue gathers information on most valuable items in the collections of Belarusian museums.

Multimedia complex dedicated to the life and work of Francysk Skaryna, a high-tech layout version of the Francysk Skaryna Bible and the augmented reality glasses, depicting 3D versions of the Kreva and Halshany Castles are among the technical innovations of our museum.

Institute of Nasledie (Stravropol) Ltd.

Founded in 1995, the institute's activities encompass archaeological research of historical and cultural monuments, identification of historical and cultural monuments in the areas zoned out for development and construction, conservation of antiquities and archaeological textiles, development and deployment of geo-information technologies for archaeological research. The institute is involved in a wide array of international partnerships ranging from joint archaeological excavations to genomic research of the population of ancient Eurasia.

National Museum in Belgrade, Serbia

The National Museum in Belgrade is a complex museum. It is the largest, oldest and central museum of Serbia, which, after its long existence, since its founding in distant 1844, has 34 archeological, numismatic, artistic and historical collections today and preserves more than 450,000 objects that make up a unique cultural heritage of Serbia, the Central Balkans, and Europe.

Dedicated to protection, interpretation and promotion of a multi-layered cultural heritage of Serbia and the region, the National Museum in Belgrade interprets historical and contemporary cultures, serving as a source of knowledge and an active learning center in the community. The Museum was and will continually be the most important museology center in the Balkans, and a national cultural center with regional and global significance.

National Museum of China

The National Museum of China (NMC) is China's supreme establishment that acquires, collects, preserves, displays and interprets China's excellent traditional culture, revolutionary culture and advanced socialist culture. The NMC is the top palace of history and art and a cultural lounge for China. Led by General Secretary Xi Jinping, all members of the Standing Committee of the 18th CPC Central Committee Political Bureau visited NMC's permanent exhibition *The Road of Rejuvenation* on November 29, 2012. During that visit, General Secretary Xi Jinping called for realizing the Chinese Dream of the great rejuvenation of the Chinese nation, ushering in the new era of socialism with Chinese characteristics.

The National Museum of China houses more than 1.4 million items of collection, covering ancient and modern artifacts, rare and antiquarian books, and works of art. With a floor space of nearly 200,000 square meters and 48 galleries, it is the largest single-building museum in the world. The museum has three exhibition series that consist of permanent, thematic and temporary exhibitions. It constitutes an exhibition system covering permanent and thematic exhibitions, as well as exhibitions featuring major themes, selected historical collections, archaeological discoveries, classical artworks, regional cultures and international exchanges. The number of visitors reached a record high in 2018, with over 8.61 million visitors, making the NMC one of the most visited museums in the world.

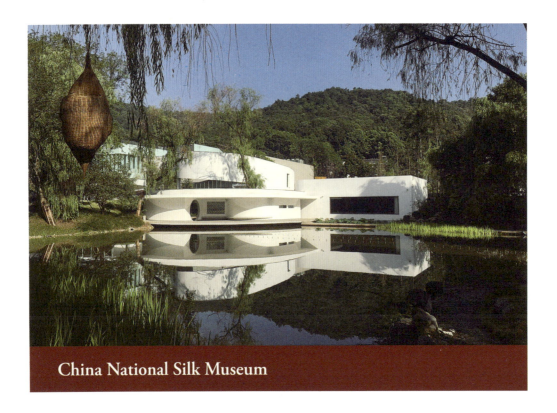

China National Silk Museum

China National Silk Museum was opened first in Feb. 1992 and reopened after the renovation in Sept. 2016. It is now a national first-grade museum encompassing textile and garment cultural heritage collection, protection, research, exhibition, inheritance and innovation with Chinese silk as the core. The display area covers 10,000 square meters, divided into six galleries, in a typical southern Chinese garden of 40,000 square meters. There are the Silk Road Gallery, the Sericulture and the Weaving Galleries, the Textile Conservation Gallery, the Fashion Gallery and Xinyou Archive Center for display. There are also Brocade Cafe, Jingluntang World Silk Boutique, NSM shop in the museum offering drinks, books, souvenirs and silk products.

Fujian Museum

As one of the national first-grade museums, Fujian Museum was established in 1933, and was rebuilt in the West Lake Park of Fuzhou, Fujian Province in 2002. Fujian Museum is the only six-in-one comprehensive museum in China combining a museum, Natural Science Center, Jicuiyuan Gallery, Institute of Archaeology, Cultural Relics Conservation Center and National Underwater Archeology Research Base. It houses over 280,000 various objects and artifacts highlighted with 30,000 rare collections. The museum have seven permanent exhibitions including *Splendid Civilization of Ancient Fujian*, *Splendor of Fujian Opera*, *Rare Crafts*, *Archeology Research Outcome*, *Splendor of Maritime Silk Road*, *Dinosaurs World* and *Natural World*. Besides, the museum also presents more than 30 temporary exhibitions.

Fujian museum has made innovative efforts in curation, branding, academic research and management model, which has achieved significant results. As the only award-winning state-owned museum, it won the Award for Most Innovative Museums in 2015. It also won the excellence of the most innovative, inspirational and awarded project in the field of museums,

heritage and conservation in 2016. Moreover, it has been invited to enjoy the permanent membership of the Best in Heritage's Excellence Club. As the only museum representative in the world, it was invited to participate in the seminar hosted by the United Nations Headquarters in Vienna and to make a speech on the Long Maritime Silk Road at the seminar.

Xi'an Tang West Market Museum

The Xi'an Tang West Market Museum, founded on the site of the West Market of the Tang Chang'an city, the eastern terminal of the Silk Road, is the first private on-the-site museum in China reflecting the Silk Road culture and business culture. The collection of the museum has now expanded to a total of more than 20,000 objects. The exhibits on display reflect a long history over 3,000 years ranging from the Shang and Zhou dynasties to the Ming and Qing dynasties. The collection includes exquisite and mysterious bronze wares, splendid and colorful ceramics, terra-cotta figurines with rich postures, brilliant gold and silver wares, gorgeous and delicate silk remains, and jade pieces of wonderful workmanship, as well as a great number of relics such as money, epitaphs, religious and architectural items, which lays a solid foundation for magnificent exhibitions. It is the first and only national first-grade museum among all the non-state museums in China so far.

图书在版编目（ＣＩＰ）数据

丝绸之路国际博物馆联盟首届联盟大会文集 ： 汉英
对照 / 王春法主编 . -- 北京 ： 朝华出版社，2021.4
　　ISBN 978-7-5054-4563-5

　　Ⅰ．①丝… Ⅱ．①王… Ⅲ．①博物馆学－文集－汉、
英 Ⅳ．① G260-53

中国版本图书馆 CIP 数据核字 (2019) 第 282809 号

丝绸之路国际博物馆联盟首届联盟大会文集

主　　编　王春法

责任编辑　吴　晶
特约编辑　刘小磊
责任印制　陆竞赢
出版发行　朝华出版社
社　　址　北京市西城区百万庄大街 24 号　　　邮政编码　100037
订购电话　（010）68996050 68996522
传　　真　（010）88415258（发行部）
联系版权　zhbq@cipg.org.cn
网　　址　http://zhcb.cipg.org.cn
印　　刷　天津图文方嘉印刷有限公司
经　　销　全国新华书店
开　　本　787mm×1092mm　1/16　　　　字　　数　80 千字
印　　张　17
版　　次　2021 年 4 月第 1 版　2021 年 4 月第 1 次印刷
书　　号　ISBN 978-7-5054-4563-5
定　　价　228.00 元